An Army *in* Heaven

KELLEY JANKOWSKI

PAGE PUBLISHING, INC.
New York, NY

First originally published by Page Publishing, Inc. 2016

ISBN 978-1-68213-182-4 (pbk)
ISBN 978-1-68213-183-1 (digital)

Printed in the United States of America

To my dear husband Ron, who is the best man I know—thank you for so many wonderful years of love and encouragement. To our beautiful children, Nicole, Sean "Halo", Anthony, Bernadette, Abbey and Susan, who have always told me to write my patient's stories down. Thank you too for your technical and artistic expertise. For my brother Sean McDermott, who so willingly helped me edit page after page, and for his sound spiritual guidance. For my brother Pat McDermott, who unknowingly gave me the name of this book, and is always ready with a kind word. To my dear friend Bobbie Norris, who told me when I started hospice nursing to "keep a journal". And mostly, to my dear patients, my faithful departed, whose lives and experiences shaped me as a nurse and show me every day, that the best is yet to come.

> *"Remember that when you leave this earth you can take nothing of what you have received, only what you have given: a full heart, enriched by honest service, love, sacrifice, and courage".*
> *St. Francis of Assisi*

Contents

Frank: Together Since Age Six

Early in my nursing career, one of the first patients whose death I witnessed was a man named Frank. He was a seventy-two-year-old Italian man who came to our hospital in the early 1980s for an aortic valve replacement. He had an extensive list of other medical conditions, which made him a huge surgical risk, and post-op, Frank developed complication after complication. He had to go back to surgery once, then developed a severe infection that debilitated him, but it did eventually clear up. His kidneys, having struggled through two surgeries, infection, and years of diabetes, began to fail. Opting not to do dialysis and nearly a month in the hospital, he finally decided to stop all further invasive medical interventions. He was made a DNR (do not resuscitate) and was placed on comfort measures. He was maintained on our step-down unit and placed on comfort care.

Frank was rather short, solid, and stocky in build, with thick, wavy salt-and-pepper hair that hadn't receded much for a man in his early seventies. His olive-toned skin showed signs of sun damage from years of working in the fields on his farm. He and his beloved wife, Maria, met in the first grade when her family moved to town from New York, and they have been inseparable since. They dated all through high school and married the summer after graduation.

Maria was a petite, slender woman with long gray hair pinned neatly up on top of her head. Her very thick glasses made her pale-blue eyes much larger in appearance. Her face, wrinkled and rent with sorrow, revealed years of hard work and yet was distinctly beautiful. Although she and Frank were never able to have children, she spoke about all their "summer sons," who were hired during spring planting to help at the farmers' market then returned in the fall at bailing and harvesttime before school began. Maria stayed at Frank's bedside during his entire stay in the hospital, doting over his every need. She would often run her fingers through his thick mass of hair, humming softly until he fell asleep. She was a very soft-spoken, gracious woman, who perpetually thanked us for any kindness shown to her or her beloved spouse.

Frank, congenial and a gentleman up to the end, had forged many relationships with the staff, and we all loved him. He declined to the point that he was in and out of consciousness. For many hours, Maria sat next to him fingering her rosary beads, deep in prayer, with her other hand resting in his. We all did our best to console and support Maria, but she was often heard from the hallway softly sobbing next to his bed. This was very difficult to hear as we all loved her and empathized with her pain. When time permitted during my shifts, I often sat next to her and prayed with her when she asked me to. She spoke about the people who had sent each of the numerous bouquets of flowers and plants, as well as the countless letters received from all over their home state. She read the letters over and over, amazed that each one contained a story unknown to her about her husband. She learned through them that he often quietly supported many large families in the area, delivering bushels of produce to help them through the tough times while never asking for any pay. His deliveries, at times, were made in the middle of the night, if he learned of a family too embarrassed to ask for his assistance.

"Frankie never told me about all of this, there's just so many families! Just look at this pile of letters!" She stood up and lifted the large basket filled to the brim with cards and letters, and sat back down next to me. She was obviously moved as her wrinkled hands caressed the top of the pile. "Years and years of good deeds, most

8

of which I'd never heard about. Oh, Frankie, you were such a good man." She stood back up and placed the basket back on the counter, then leaned over and kissed his forehead as he slept.

One evening, Frank's breathing became more labored and congested. Despite medications, nebulizer treatments, and other drugs to ease congestion, his breathing grew more difficult. With every inhalation, the all-too-familiar death rattle became louder. Maria often smothered his face with kisses, telling him, "It's time, Frankie, it's time . . . Go on home to God." At other times, she would lay her head across his chest; her tears dampening the front of his hospital gown as she listened intently to the clicks of his artificial heart valve. Maria and I were sitting together this particular evening, and I was finding it very difficult to fight back the tears when, suddenly, Frank opened up his eyes and looked directly at Maria. She got up, leaned over him, and said, "What is it, darling? What can I do?"

Frank's eyes were sunken, dark-rimmed, and exhausted, but they remained fixed on Maria's. She put her hands on each side of his face and kissed his forehead. "Oh, Frankie, it'll be all right. You just let go, I'll be okay."

A single tear seeped out of Frank's right eye, which she gently and lovingly wiped away. Frank's gaze remained steady as the life in his eyes slowly ebbed away, and they lost their luster, becoming dull and glazed as he took his final breaths. Maria reached up when his chest became silent and still, and slowly closed his eyelids. Then kissing each eye, she whispered, "I will love you forever and ever." She began to cry.

I gave her time alone with him until she emerged from his room, her suitcase in hand. She hugged the staff and thanked us profusely for caring for her husband. She asked that the bouquets of flowers and plants be given to other patients who didn't have any. "Frank would have wanted it that way." She smiled, turned, and slowly walked out of the unit, hunched over and heavy with grief.

Mabel: A Cruel Memory

Mabel was a woman who had been admitted into our unit after suffering a massive heart attack. Her heart had suffered a series of small attacks over the years due to noncompliant control of her diabetes and hypertension, but this final one would prove fatal. She entered our ICU from the ER, intubated and connected to a ventilator. After countless attempts to locate her family, we were finally able to locate a daughter named Joelle. We updated her about her mother's condition, but she opted not to come in. In fact, none of Mabel's children came in for the week she was with us.

During our phone conversation, while we were discussing the code status of her mother, Joelle said, "No, don't do anything else to prolong this. If she goes, just let her go." With that said, the resident was put on the phone and the verbal consent for DNR was obtained, and comfort measures were initiated.

Mabel took a turn for the worse that morning around four o'clock, so I notified Joelle to see if she wanted to come in to be with her mother. "Just let me know when she dies," Joelle said before hanging up the phone. I thought this a rather strange response, but then many don't have the stomach or the heart to handle seeing their loved ones hooked up to so many machines. I didn't linger on the whats and whys of the situation but told her I would let her know.

Mabel passed shortly after 5:00 AM, and I was alone in the room with her when she died. Standing next to her bed, I felt a disturbing sensation. A palpable eerie feeling in the room that made the hair on the back of my neck bristle. Left with this uneasy feeling, I called another nurse to help me prepare her body for the family. When we removed the breathing tube and the straps holding it in place, Mabel's face was twisted, clenched, with an indelible frown on her face. We attempted everything to soften her appearance—repositioning her head, combing her hair, and bathing her face—but nothing helped soften her tortured and furrowed expression. The other nurse stated she didn't want to stay in the room any longer and left.

"What? Where are you going? We're not finished," I said.

"There's something not right in here, and it's giving me the creeps! I'll get somebody else to help you," she replied, and darted out of the room. In her defense, she was absolutely right, and her refusal to stay in the room with me confirmed that what I sensed was in fact a palpable phenomenon. The replacement nurse arrived, and we quickly finished our duties, and she also felt the strange eeriness in the room.

When the post-mortem care was completed, I awaited Joelle's arrival. She arrived an hour later, and when she entered Mabel's room, she looked at her mother and, in a detached and rather cold tone, said, "Well, she's finally dead."

"Were you close to your mother?" I asked, almost out of curiosity to maybe explain her aloof statement.

"No, no, I wasn't." She hesitated for a moment and then continued, "My mother was one nasty woman. She was cruel and never should have been allowed to be a mother. All of us feel the same way. As soon as we were old enough, we were out of that house. No matter how many times we tried to make her happy and to be good kids, she dished out nothing but hatred. Day after day, we were forced to listen to terrible cruelty from her foul, cussin' mouth. And don't get too close to her during one of her rampages because if she caught us, we were whipped with an old purse strap or a metal spatula until we were covered in welts."

Joelle proceeded to tell of her life growing up and the bizarre and moody behavior of the woman she called mother. She spoke of her four other siblings and how they all had struggled to lead normal lives once they left home and were out of their mother's grip. I let her vent as she retold episode after episode of abuse and neglect. As she continued, there was a struggle in her voice, as if she were choking back tears and anger, tangled with so much unfinished business and unsaid words between them. In one protracted tale of pain, she divulged the memories of a broken and battered childhood.

"Oh, Joelle, that's awful. I can't imagine how difficult it must have been for all of you."

"It was hell on earth, I tell you, just hell on earth!" Joelle paused, staring at her mother's body. "But you know, our youngest brother, Billy, got the worst of it. He ran away from home when he was sixteen and was murdered a year later. He got into drugs and hooked up with a gang of kids that became his family. I've never forgotten it or forgiven my mother for it. Yes, ma'am, it was *her* fault he left home, because he took the brunt of her hatred. She really had it out for that boy." She sighed and shook her head.

"Why do you think she targeted him?" I asked.

"Well, we all think it was because he looked most like his daddy. He left when Billy was just a baby because he was carrying on with some woman down the street. Mabel never forgave him for it, so her hatred for him was thrown onto Billy instead. And no matter how we all tried to protect him, she always got to him. We were all scared to death of her." She adjusted herself, obviously uncomfortable with the memories. "But it's over now, thank God, and now she'll really see what she did to us. God will show her what a terrible impact she had on every single one of us, and she'll be forced to see it all because she sure as hell never listened to any of us."

Joelle stared at Mabel for a time, and then pointing her finger at her and choking back her tears, she said, "This was a cruel and heartless bitch of a woman, and I was ashamed to call her my mother." She stood quietly for a while, gazing at her mother lying lifeless on the bed. She had an expression on her face as though she were remember-ing, concentrating, going through the different scenarios engrained in her memory. With a start, she straightened up and looped her purse over her left forearm. She ran her fingers through the hair on either side of her face, curling it behind her ears. She turned around with her back toward her mother, and after a short pause, she looked over at me and said, "Do what you want with her body. None of us want it!" She then walked out of the unit.

Robert: Close to the Light

Robert was a forty-seven-year-old male who had come into the hospital for chest pain. According to his lab work and his EKGs, he had infarcted previously, and now his cardiac enzymes were on the decline. Since the damage was done, he was brought to our unit from the ER for close observation as he was having arrhythmias (an irregular heart rhythm).

Robert was a thin man with the beginnings of graying hair along his temples. With salt-and-pepper goatee and small spectacles, I imagined him more a professor than an IT computer technician. He had been a smoker for many years, and his sedentary job involved long hours behind a desk. I settled him into his bed, hooked him up to the array of IVs and monitors, and took his vital signs. When I finished, I went to the nurses' station to check his chart and review the rest of his orders. Within minutes, his heart monitor started alarming, and I heard him say, "I don't feel very well, I think I'm going to be sick."

I ran quickly into the room accompanied by another nurse named Terry. She grabbed an emesis bucket just as Robert began to vomit. I looked up at the monitor to see his heart rate quickly dropping in complete heart block. I ran to the emergency medication cart, grabbed Atropine, and quickly pushed it into his IV line while the CCU resident was being paged. He had lost consciousness but was still breathing. As soon as the Atropine hit his veins, his heart rate quickly picked up from 28 up to 84.

Robert shot up into a sitting position and yelled, "Is it normal to hallucinate during a heart attack?"

"Robert, your heart rate dropped, and we had to give you medicine to bring it up," I said as I wrapped the blood pressure cuff around his arm.

"Wow! Everything went dark, and I started flying through this tunnel!"

A few minutes after the CCU resident arrived, Robert shakily said again, "I don't feel very well." Immediately, his heart rate started to dip again, and Robert began to vomit. I grabbed the Atropine and started injecting it when he again lapsed into unconsciousness. We quickly set up and began prepping him for a temporary pacemaker insertion, and the resident grabbed the phone and STAT-paged the attending cardiologist. Once the Atropine took effect, Robert again woke up and asked the same questions. This time he described the distant light that he was quickly approaching. "I was almost there when I woke up here. What the hell is going on? Why am I hallucinating?"

Terry and I looked at each other in complete disbelief. "I hope his cardiologist hurries up," I whispered to her as I wet a washcloth to wipe Robert's face.

"I've never seen anything like this, going back and forth like that," she whispered back, then turned to empty the emesis basin into the toilet. When the cardiologist arrived, he quickly threw his coat on the nurses' station, grabbed Robert's chart, and darted into the room. He was updated on the situation, and Robert desperately attempted to tell him what had happened. We had everything ready for the temporary pacemaker insertion and pulled in the fluoroscopy machine. After the cardiologist finished placing the cordis and he began the insertion of the pacing wires, Robert's heart rate dropped again.

"I'm getting dizzy, and I'm getting nauseated again." The cardiologist inserted the proximal pacemaker wires into the external console I was holding, and I quickly turned it on and increased the voltage and the rate to his specifications. You could see it capture on the monitor, and it immediately started controlling Robert's heart rate, preventing it from dipping below 60. He was prepped and taken to the cardiac catheterization lab, where he had two vessels opened up by angioplasty. A permanent pacemaker was subsequently inserted due to continuing arrhythmias and symptomatic heart block. Robert arrived back into our unit and was stabilized.

I had the opportunity to care for Robert for the next two days, and after some prompting, he related his journey from the bed, through the tunnel, and toward the light.

"I knew you people thought I was hallucinating, but it was real! When everything went black I immediately felt myself pulled upward, and I was completely surrounded by darkness, a quiet and very peaceful darkness. I was travelling through a cylindrical tunnel, and the sides of the tunnel shimmered with the most beautiful blue specks of light. Some I flew past, but others travelled along with me. At the end of this tunnel was a warm golden light, and inside this light was love. The closer I got to it, the more happiness and joy I felt. This light was so beautiful and so brilliant that I knew it was God. But at the same time, the closer I came to it, I realized how completely unprepared I was to see Him face-to-face. Then immediately I was pulled backward, and I woke up here. It was so disappointing and a relief all at the same time.

"The second time I was again in the same tunnel with the same specks of light, and I was moving quickly toward that same warm light. I was almost there when that same realization that I wasn't ready hit me. I was almost to the opening where He was standing, and felt the most incredible love and warmth surround me. I heard His voice within my mind tell me that it wasn't time. Very quickly I felt myself pulled back again, and then I woke up here."

"Twice your heart rate dropped very low, and we gave you medication to pick it up until the cardiologist could put in the pacemaker," I explained, smiling at Robert as he adjusted himself in the bed.

He paused for a moment and then looked up at me and said, "I never really thought about life after death before this. I mean, I learned about God and heaven when I was a boy, but I never really practiced any sort of formal religion. I tried to be good, but that was about it. But let me tell you, if that's what it's like to die, I'm not afraid because it was the most pleasant experience of my life. And this I know more than I know anything else—that God loves me. He loves me like no one ever has, but I know I have more to do here."

"What more do you think you have to do? Did He tell you?" I asked as I finished adjusting his IV pump.

"No, He never said specifically, but I know I have to prepare myself for the rest of my life . . . my life in heaven. I know that this is my time of preparation, and it is very short. I have a lot more to do before I can meet God—meet Him for good, that is." He dropped his eyes toward his lap, fiddling with his fingernails. Smiling, he raised his head and said, "I had no idea how very good—how very, very good—God is. If I'd only known, or had any idea how much God really loved me, I would have been a better man." He paused and then smiled. He looked over at me and touched my hand and said, "But I will now."

Jessica: Drug and Child Abuse

With the ring of the telephone, another admission is to arrive from the Emergency Room. It was reported that a young woman named Jessica was being admitted with sepsis. She was running a high fever and needed a central line for antibiotics and fluids. Since the ER was massively backed up, the surgical residents opted to place the line once she was in our unit. The ER gurney rolled through the door a short time later, carrying a young woman flushed with fever. This petite, thin girl lying in the bed was barely eighteen years old, but the ravages of a difficult life were painted upon her face and reflected in her eyes. She had dark-brown hair and her dark charcoal-colored makeup was smeared from tears and sweat. Her pale-blue eyes were bloodshot and weary, and her chin shivered as her body was rigid and racked with chills. When we transferred her from the ER gurney into the bed, she grimaced in discomfort and supported her swollen, discolored left arm with her right. We quickly settled her into her bed, hooked her up to the cardiac monitor, took her vital signs, and paged the surgical resident that his patient had arrived. This young girl was a walk-in from the streets. She was a homeless girl who had infected track lines from IV drug abuse. The infection in her left arm had led to cellulitis, causing her left arm to swell almost double in size, and it was red and hot and very painful when touched. Cellulitis is a bacterial skin infection that, if left untreated, spreads to deeper tissues around the initial infected area. In Jessica's case, bacteria were introduced into her skin by dirty needles. Untreated for many weeks, the infection had now spread into her bloodstream, which would inevitably be fatal if left untreated. Since there were no peripheral veins on her right arm that weren't scarred from intravenous drug use, it was necessary to place a central line. A central line is a long large-bore IV that is placed into one of the larger veins in her neck or below her clavicle, either the internal jugular vein or the subclavian vein, respectively.

In getting Jessica prepped, the surgeon placed a sterile drape over her right shoulder and neck area, and a portion of it also draped over her head and face. She frantically sat up in the bed, ripped it off her face, threw it at the doctor, and screamed, "Damn it, you jackass! I told you a million times, don't put nothin' over my damn face. What are you? Ignorant or just stupid?" He quickly apologized, and after calmly coaxing her, we were able to lay her back down again. I retrieved a new sterile drape then stayed on the left side of the bed and talked her through everything that needed to be done. She grabbed my hand and said that when people put things over her face, she becomes so claustrophobic that "it makes me nuts inside." I told her that I would hold the drape up away from her face until the procedure finished and stay with her the entire time. She finally consented, and the procedure began.

To keep her mind off the needles of numbing medication, and the pressure and discomfort that she would inevitably feel, I talked to her about what transpired to bring her into the ER and her personal and medical history. Aside from her limited medical history, she proceeded to tell me about her life. She explained that her father died from a drug overdose when she was very small; her mother was addicted to heroin and cocaine as well as other drugs, but "her lover was definitely heroin." Widowed, depressed, and desperate, her mother's drug use escalated to the point that she could no longer afford her habit. She used to prostitute herself for money, for drugs, and often left her small daughter home alone.

"When I was eight years old, I got raped by one of my mother's johns. She walked in on it, and they started screaming at each other. He threw a wad of money in her face to shut her up. She shut up all right, but pimped me to another guy, then another, then another. I fought as hard as I could to keep those dirty pigs off of me, but she got sick of me screaming. So one night, she tied me down and shot me up to keep me quiet," Jessica said with very little emotion in her voice.

"What are you saying? Your mother injected you with drugs?" I asked in absolute disbelief.

"Yes, that's what I said! Don't tell me you're stupid too? Of course she did, because that way, she could let him do what he wanted to do without all my fightin' and screamin'. I was pimped out to all her asshole johns for money—at least the ones that was into little girls. And if they didn't have no money, they paid her in drugs."

My heart ached as the story continued, and I had to fight back the tears listening to incident after incident. I could hardly handle hearing of the hell this poor child went through, and finally, I couldn't stop it and tears rolled down my cheeks.

"What the hell you bawlin' for? Didn't happen to you!" she snapped.

"I don't know how you handled that—"

"You wanna hear my story, or is you just gonna bawl?"

"No, please go on, I want to hear your story." I grabbed a tissue and wiped my eyes, then straightened up to get my composure.

"One pig used to show up for me all the time, and if I cried or made any sounds, he'd shove a pillow over my face, so I learned real quick to shut my damn mouth."

"Oh my goodness, Jessica, that's why you couldn't handle the drape . . . I'm so sorry."

"I can't breathe, and I get all freaked out inside." Her eyes began to well up with tears. I tried to wipe her eyes, but she impatiently said, "I can do it myself." So I put a tissue in her left hand, and she lifted her swollen arm up to her face to wipe her tears. In a quiet whisper, she said, "Now you f—— ing get it?" The surgical resident raised his eyebrows and looked over at me.

20

"I'm so sorry, I had no idea. How did you escape from that?" I asked in an attempt to redirect and change to something less heartbreaking.

"I've been out on the streets on and off since I been 'bout fourteen years old." (Well, that idea obviously didn't work.)

"You were still a baby!"

"Well, the streets is better than hell" she said abruptly.

"What about foster care? Social workers? Did you ever tell anyone what happened to you?"

"When I was 'bout ten years old, I accidentally locked myself out of the house one mornin', and somebody called and reported it. I guess seein' me dressed in filthy rags and not havin' a bath clued 'em in. I was put in foster care that same day, and when the doctors checked me over and saw the marks on my arms and the condition of my lady parts, they arrested her. I never went back home after that. I didn't have to tell them anything, my body said enough. They put that bitch away, and I didn't see her for years." She smirked. "They got a hold of two of the bastards that raped me too. Didn't get all of 'em, but two is better than none."

"Do you know where your mom is now, or is she still in jail?" I asked.

"About a year ago, I heard she got outta prison and was livin' in some halfway house, so I decided to go and let her have it. I was plannin' on telling her exactly what I thought of her, but I didn't. She's got AIDS now, and she looked like shit . . . just a damn bag o' bones, so I didn't say nothin' to her. I stood in the corner and just stared at her. She walked up to me, wanted to bum a smoke, so I gave her one and handed her my lighter. I looked right at her, but she didn't recognize me, and I never told her who I was neither. She's gettin' what she deserves." Her eyes glanced away, and I could tell she was uncomfortable talking about it.

"What about your foster homes?"

"Why the hell you wanna know all that for? Fine . . . I was in and outta foster homes, but none of them was where I wanted to be . . . they didn't really want me." Jessica paused, moved her gaze away, then whispered, "Nobody ever wanted me."

"But how do you survive on the streets? How do you live and eat?"

"You do what you gotta to do. You meet people and figure out the ones you can trust and the ones who's just crazy. I got a friend I hang with, and he keeps them crazy ones away from me."

"I wish there was something we could do to help you."

"You're so full of crap. I'm just a stupid kid who's been dumped on my whole life. Sure ain't nothing you can do, not sure what don't you understand 'bout that?" She looked away for a moment. "Most times, I just wish I was dead, 'specially in winter, like now, when it's so freakin' cold. Ain't nobody out there anywhere who gives a damn 'bout some strung-out kid who never amounted to nothin'. He about done? Because I'm about to lose it!" she said as the anxiety rose in her voice.

The surgical resident had just finished suturing the line in place and was putting a sterile dressing over it. After the chest X-ray to check placement, the IV fluids and the antibiotics were started. I bathed her and washed her hair, and the basin of water had to be changed five times as the filth from the streets slowly washed away. Underneath was a young woman whose face looked much older than her stated age, and other than the scarred marks on her arms, the rest of her skin still had the youthful appearance of an eighteen-year-old. She stabilized and left our unit a few days later and was moved to a medical floor. I had initiated a social-work consult the night she arrived, but lost track of her. I never saw Jessica again but think of her often and the abuse she'd suffered. If this was her springboard into life, the poor girl never had a chance from the very beginning.

Gracie: Unable to Let Go

Gracie was admitted into the Critical Care Unit at 11:00 PM from the ER with hypotension, respiratory failure, and stage IV metastatic colon cancer. She had a bowel obstruction, as the cancer invading the intestine had completely blocked it. According to the ER nurse's report, when they passed a nasogastric tube into her nose, down her esophagus and into her stomach, they removed almost two liters of bile and gastric fluid. When this very tiny woman rolled through the door, her condition was shocking. She weighed 78 pounds and was intubated and connected to a ventilator that regulated every breath she received. She had a fine layer of white hair resembling peach fuzz that was growing back in from chemo. A central line in her left subclavian was connected to several IV medications to help elevate her blood pressure, and yet her blood pressure was still dangerously low. She had very little urine output, and you could see tumors visibly bulging beneath her frail, thin skin. When we rolled her onto her side to remove the ER linens from underneath her, she had noticeable tumors over the posterior portion of her back. She had a large bedsore on the sacral area, which had eroded through her skin and down through the subcutaneous tissues to the bone. We cleaned and dressed the wound and rolled her onto her side to relieve the pressure off her bedsore, as bedsores are always very painful.

"This poor woman!" said one of the other nurses as she looked at Gracie. "She's in really bad shape."

"Her husband can't let her go, according to the ER report," I told her.

"Well, it won't be very long, and he won't have a choice. Look at her blood pressure and her heart rate! She looks like she'll break if we even touch her!"

When I looked over at the contents of what the nasogastric tube was removing from her stomach, and disconnected it get a better look, it was immediately obvious that this was much more than bile and gastric fluid. There was liquid stool draining from her gut. Her intestinal obstruction was so complete that even stool couldn't pass and had backed up all the way into her stomach. She had little to no muscle mass left and was literally a skeleton covered with skin. Her abdomen was very distended and hard, and she looked like a woman nine months pregnant. When we finished settling her in, I walked out of the room and asked the medical resident sitting at the desk if anyone had spoken to the husband about a code status. Without looking up from the computer monitor, his response was brief, "Yes, we did, but he didn't want to hear it."

"I think you should try again because she's not going to make it. She really doesn't have long."

Without looking up, he impatiently replied, "As I said, three of us tried, and he didn't want to discuss it."

"Do you mind if I go speak to him?" I asked as I leaned on the counter.

"Knock yourself out, but he's not going to give his consent to *you*," he said, still looking at the computer screen.

I left Gracie in the care of the other nurses and went into the waiting room to speak with her husband. I found him sitting alone in the empty waiting room, his head in his hands with his elbows resting on his knees. I slipped into the chair next to him and put my hand on his shoulder. He lifted his head, looked at me, and said, "Is she still alive?"

"Yes, she is, but I'm afraid it doesn't look good. Her blood pressure is very low, and the medications we are giving her aren't able to get it back up. How long has your wife been ill?"

He proceeded to tell me from the day of her diagnosis up to the present, three long and arduous years. He sighed, wiped his tears with the palm of his hand, and said, "Please don't let her die." Then he broke down, weeping into his hands.

"I can't imagine how difficult this must be for you, but there's something you need to understand about the condition that Gracie's in." He sobbed, took a deep breath, and looked up at me, tears streaming down his face. "Gracie's cancer is well beyond the point that anyone can do anything about, you're aware of that, yes?" I asked. He nodded his reply. "All of the medications, tubes, and machines can no longer do anything to stop it, and that's where we are right now—that's where Gracie is right now. We are no longer prolonging her life, but are only prolonging her death. She's near the end of her journey, and there's very little we can do for her, except to keep her comfortable," I said as gently as I could.

"What do I do then? What do I do now? What am I going to do without her?" he said, clinching his hands together. He broke down, heaving with every sob, snot and tears streaming from his face. I grabbed a tissue and gave it to him, and he wiped his tears and blew his nose. Every sentence was an effort, every word difficult to get out between the jerking inhalations from prolonged crying.

Slowly I said to him, "Go in to Gracie, hold her hand, kiss her, tell her you love her and that it's okay. Tell her it's okay to go to God, and most importantly, tell her that *you* are going to be okay."

"You're talking about making her a DNR, aren't you? That won't scare her?" he piped in, looking up at me with so much worry across his face.

"She may be hanging on because she needs to hear that you'll be okay," I said as I handed him another tissue.

"I don't want her to suffer anymore, I really don't. She has suffered for so long, but I love her so much," he said as his sobbing began again. "But if I make her a DNR, that means I gave up on her.

I don't ever want her to think I gave up because I would never give up on my Gracie!"

"You're not giving up, just focusing more on keeping her comfortable until her time comes. Gracie is tired . . . she has lost the strength to fight this cancer." I squeezed his hands and he looked up at me. "Are you sure she won't think I'm giving up? I don't want to pull the plug, but I don't want her hurting either. What do I do?" he asked with added worry in his voice.

"We aren't going to pull anything, but we can add medication to ease her pain, help her breathing, ease any anxiety that may be going on inside. But if her heart stops, we won't jump in and pound on her chest or put any more tubes in. When God calls, we'll just simply let her go to Him."

"Can she still hear me?" he asked with hopeful anticipation.

"Hearing is the last sense that we relinquish, so she can absolutely still hear you." I stood up and put out my hand and helped him up from his chair.

We walked into the unit and went into Gracie's room. He went up to her bedside, and I lowered the side rail so he could get close to her. I moved the tubes and the IV poles out of his way and encouraged him to hold her, to touch her. He put his left arm behind her head and her shoulders, and cradled her as he kissed her forehead, stroking her face and hair with his other hand.

"Gracie, it's me, honey, I'm here. I know that you can hear me, sweetheart." He rocked her gently back and forth, patting her gently as he cradled her, very much like a mother does to soothe her child, showering her face and forehead with kisses. "Gracie, listen to me, my darling. If you need to go, you just go ahead and go. It's okay . . . it's okay. I don't want you hurting anymore, and I know that you're tired. You go ahead of me and wait for me, okay, sweetheart? I'll see you again, I will and . . . I'll be all right."

He sobbed out the words, stopping and repeating them to make sure she heard clearly what he was saying. I closed the curtain and slowly shut the glass doors so he could whisper all those tender things a husband needs to tell his wife in a situation like this. I waited outside the cubicle for about ten minutes. I told the medical resident that Gracie's husband was ready to give the DNR consent. He looked up from his computer and finally made eye contact.

"What? How did you convince him of that?"

"I told him the truth, that his wife was dying and there was nothing anyone could do." I reached into the file cabinet next to him and handed him the DNR form.

When Gracie's husband appeared from behind the curtains, his grief was evident, but he was more peaceful. The resident gave him the consent form to sign for "comfort measures only." When we returned to Gracie's room, I set him up in a chair to keep his final vigil at her bedside. I kept the side rail down to make it easier for him to touch her, hold her hand, and whisper into her ears all that he held in his heart. We continued the IV fluids and medications, but did not increase them. A very small dose of morphine was added to calm her breathing since she was struggling, breathing forty-four times a minute. After the first dose, her struggling and gasping respirations eased, and her furrowed brow softened; her face became relaxed and serene. Gracie's husband and I sat at her bedside on and off throughout the shift, talking. He opened up about his wife and the good times they had together, and his face lit up as he reviewed their lifetime of memories. He spoke about God and heaven. He marveled how she would get to see her parents and two brothers again, as she had ached for them since their passing. He never let go of her hand, and she never required another dose of morphine and passed into eternity at 7:04 AM with her husband at her side.

Harry: Invisible Visitors

"Why are you in my damn house? Get the hell out of here! I didn't say you could come in!" Harry yelled at the top of his lungs. That's how the night began when I went into his room to introduce myself.

Harry was a seventy-eight-year-old man whose dementia had advanced to the point where he could no longer safely stay home alone. He was an overflow patient sent to our unit until a bed opened up on the medical floor. There were no beds to be had on this particular summer night, and the hospital was running at capacity. Harry had been married fifty-two years, until his wife Margie passed eight months previously. He drastically declined after her death, and it was obvious that she was the glue that held him together, his link to reality and familiarity. This particular evening, Harry was found wandering up and down the sidewalk, very confused and yelling at people to "get off my property!" Bystanders called 911, and when officers arrived with an ambulance, he was initially angry and combative until they told him they were taking him to see Margie. He was then brought to our hospital for evaluation. It was discovered that electrolyte imbalances and poor nutrition had sent him into a tailspin.

"Get outta here, damn it! You deaf?" he screamed at me.

"But, Harry, I'm here to make you something to eat, are you hungry?" I asked nonchalantly.

"I'm starving! Damn people keep coming in here and stealing my food. You gonna make me something?" he snapped.

"Well, I can't go for groceries until tomorrow, but I could make you a sandwich, is that okay?" I asked, hoping he would agree.

"I'll eat anything. Check the fridge and bring me something, and hurry up about it." I was dismissed with the wave of his hand. I went into the little kitchenette on the unit, knowing full well that we don't keep much of anything as far as food. I fixed him a jelly sandwich and brought in three puddings, graham crackers, a small bowl of fruit, and a cold Ensure. When I walked back into his room, he yelled again for me to get out of his house.

"But, Harry, I made you something to eat. I bet you're hungry, aren't you?"

"Damn right I'm hungry! What 'ya got?" he asked, wiping away the items on the over-bed table in front of him, not flinching as they cascaded to the floor and evicted their contents as they crashed against the tile. I set up the sandwich and other goodies on his bedside table and poured his Ensure into a cup. After I cleaned up the floor, I sat at the edge of the bed while Harry ravenously ate.

"So how have you been, Harry? It's awful good to see you again," I asked in a calm voice.

"Where's my wife? I can't find my wife. Margie! Margie! Where did that woman go? She's always out doing something and leaving me behind," he said in between bites.

"Margie is out running errands today, but she sent me here to help you until she gets back," I said as I poured the last bit of Ensure into his cup.

"Well, I don't want to stay here. These people aren't my kind, and I'm not comfortable here with them," he said as he jutted a finger toward the glass door of his room.

"What do you mean, Harry?"

"You see them people over there?" he mumbled through the food in his mouth, pointing at the nurses' station.

"Which ones?" I asked, leaning in to see where he was pointing.

"The ones right there where them blinking lights are," he said, pointing again and stretching his arm farther toward the door, his other hand busily shoving a spoonful of pudding into his mouth. When I looked out, I saw the cubicle across the empty nurses' station where a patient was lying in bed and the blinking lights of his IV pump were flashing, showing that the pump was functioning properly. The two green lights were blinking almost in unison.

"Okay, Harry, I see them. Why are you uncomfortable with them? They seem pretty quiet to me."

"Well, they gotta be rich, very, very rich," he replied in a rolling tone.

"What makes you think that?"

"They have a stone bust of Caesar, and its tits are blinking lights at me. That must have cost them a fortune! I don't have money like that! I need to get back to my own damn house and my own kind!" he said as busily shoved the last bit of his sandwich into his mouth.

Throughout the night, Harry often looked toward different sounds in the unit and began speaking to people who weren't in the room. He often had long conversations with people he said were "visiting" him, sitting on the windowsill or on the countertop at the foot of his bed. He often saw Margie, who came to visit, and when Margie was there, he would initially become very upset. He would yell at her, saying, "Margie, where the hell have you been woman? I've been waiting for you all damn day!" The conversation soon quieted down, and she often stayed for hours. Although invisible to us, she was very visible to Harry and kept him company. Harry was transferred to the step-down unit and was later admitted into a local nursing home. He died three weeks later from a massive stroke.

James: A Welcomed Visitor

James was a seventy-nine-year-old man who had a long history of hypertension and diabetes. His kidneys were now significantly compromised from long-term disease, and they were failing more every day. James had been in our unit a few days when he told the doctor, "I'm tired, and I don't want to do this anymore." After discussing all the options—dialysis, a change in medication—James was adamant that he was finished fighting and was ready to "go home to God."

When I first entered his room, I found an alert elderly, slightly heavy man lying peacefully in bed. He was lying on his back with his hands folded together across his abdomen. He was a handsome man who didn't look anywhere near his age as his hair had only has sparse areas of gray. He had large deep-brown eyes that were full of quiet dignity, but lit up when he smiled. After completing his physical assessment and taking his vital signs, James said, "Boy, what are you doin' here?"

I looked over at James, and he was smiling and looking at the foot of his bed. "Who are you talking to James?" I asked, since I saw no one sitting at the foot of the bed.

He looked up at me with a puzzled and impatient look on his face and said, "What, you blind woman? I'm talking to Benny right there!" He pointed to the foot of his bed.

"Oh, sorry, Benny, didn't see you slip in. Well, you two have a nice visit, and here's your call bell—you call me if you need anything at all." I placed the call bell in his hand, smiled at him as I squeezed his hand, and left the room. For over an hour and a half, James had a pleasant and animated conversation with Benny, who stayed at the foot of the bed. The nurses and I watched from the nurses' station through the glass doors as James continued speaking to this invisible visitor.

"Who is he talking to?" Mary asked as their conversation continued.

"Somebody named Benny, who is apparently sitting at the foot of the bed. I didn't want to ask who he was."

"Well, he sure sees somebody," Mary replied, smiling. "Maybe Benny's dead?"

"Probably, but whoever it is, he's enjoying his company."

When I entered the room to redo his vital signs and give him his medications, I repositioned James onto his side, rubbed his back, and positioned a pillow behind him. His blood pressure was low, and I noticed his heart rhythm becoming more irregular. James stated how tired he was, and I told him that it was good that Benny was there to visit.

"Benny's done and gone now. It sure was good seeing that boy again, so good." James smiled as I fluffed his pillow. "It's been a long time since I've seen him."

As the hours passed, James became weaker and more lethargic as his blood pressure was on a steady decline. I phoned the family and told them that it would be a good idea to come to the hospital as James was getting weaker, and I felt it wouldn't be long. When I went back into the room to tell James that his wife and children were coming, James was barely responsive, and he quickly became completely unresponsive. His heart rate was slowing, dragging his blood pressure with it, and I hoped and prayed that his family would make it in time. I stayed with James for quite some time, then I went to the nurses' station and phoned the family again, but there was no answer. Nearly an hour had passed and his family hadn't arrived. I was worried that something had happened to them when I heard the central cardiac monitor alarm. I looked up and saw that his heart rate was quickly dropping. I went into his room and picked up his hand, bent over him and whispered into his ear, "Hang on a little longer, James, your family is on their way. Just a little longer, honey, they're really wanting to see you."

Slowly his heart rate dropped further, and his rhythm changed, becoming wider and wider, and within a minute, it slipped into asystole. A few agonal breaths, and James died very quietly, very peacefully. I phoned the resident to have him come and formally pronounce James dead, as was our unit's policy. After the resident left, I removed all the IV lines and prepared James's body, bathed his face and put a clean gown and sheet on him, and waited for his family to arrive.

Shortly after, I heard the call buzzer from the outside of our locked unit, and seeing through the glass that his family had arrived, I walked to the door to let them in. When I told them that James had passed just a short while ago, they became very upset that they had missed it. They explained there was a massive car accident on the way that had stopped traffic for miles. I took them into the cubicle and closed the glass doors. The sound of their grief escalated, and we heard wave after wave of wailing emanating from his cubicle. Even with the doors closed, the crescendo of their cries was upsetting the rest of the patients in the unit. I grabbed his chart and re-entered the room, shutting the glass doors behind me. I was immediately met with a barrage of questions about when and how, and how come we didn't bring him back. I explained to them that James had requested that he not be brought back and showed them his signed consent for "comfort measures only." They argued among themselves, which only escalated, until they began getting angry. James' wife stood by the bed, holding her husband's hand, quiet in her grief. I interrupted the noise, and I asked the group if their father knew anyone named Benny.

"What? What did you say?" they all asked in near unison.

"Did James know anyone named Benny?" I repeated.

"Why do you want to know that?" one woman asked.

"Several hours ago, when I began my shift and came in to introduce myself to James, he began speaking to someone I couldn't see named Benny."

There was a long pause as they all looked at me with complete disbelief on their faces. Then his wife broke her silence and said, "Benny was our grandson who was killed four years ago in a terrible motorcycle accident—he was killed instantly. James, well, he loved that boy, loved him so much. He hasn't been the same since Benny died." She sighed.

"Well, for the last two hours that James was awake, he was visiting with Benny, who was sitting right here at the foot of his bed." I patted the spot on the bed.

"That was my son, Benny was my son." I looked over and saw a woman in her early forties who was looking at me with tears streaming down her face. A soft smile grew on her lips and she said, "I wish I would have been here." Her husband put his arm around her and held her close.

Slowly the atmosphere in the room changed, and they smiled as they remembered Benny and the special relationship that James shared with him. When they left, they were still very sad, but calm and more peaceful, knowing that Benny had come to retrieve James and ready him for his journey to heaven.

Richard: Returned for a Final Farewell

Richard was diagnosed with congestive heart failure many years ago and had been a "frequent flyer" into our unit. He often required IV medications to pull off the massive amounts of fluid that would build up in his legs and back up into his lungs.

This particular admission found him pale and much weaker than normal. Richard had a loving family and a wife who rarely left his side. He had two grown children and four grandchildren. When I arrived at work that evening, the nurse reporting off to me told me that Richard was now a DNR, and we were awaiting a private room to open up on the seventh floor. I was told that he was unconscious and had slipped into a coma two nights ago, and that the family had gone home to get some much-needed rest. Richard was my second patient, so I went in to assess and check on my first patient in the room next to his. When I finished, I walked to the nurses' station, and as I passed Richard's room, I glanced up to find him still lying on his right side, but he was looking at me. I went into the room and walked up to his bed. He followed me with his eyes, so I leaned over his bed, put my hand on his arm and said, "Well, hello, Richard! We've been wanting you to wake up." I gave him a big smile.

He smiled back and asked, "Where is my wife?"

"She went home to catch up on some sleep. Are you okay?"

"I need you to call my wife and kids and tell them to come here. They need to come here now!" he asked with such an insistence in his weak voice.

I went to the nurses' station and phoned his wife and told her what had just happened. I told her what Richard had requested and she said hurriedly, "I'm on my way, I'm on my way," and hung up the phone. I returned to Richard's room and assessed him head to toe. He had no pain and said he had no difficulty breathing. I asked him if there was anything I could do for him.

"Could you raise my head up and put me on my back so I can see my family?"

"Gladly!" I said, and proceeded to reposition him. I raised the head of his bed and freshened up his face and dampened his hair and combed it smooth. I removed his dentures and scrubbed them, rinsed out his mouth and put his clean dentures back in. As soon as I finished and was putting his basin and things away, his wife walked in. She had apparently stepped right out of her bed and into her coat and rushed over. She was in sweat pants with slippers on her feet. Her hair was disheveled, and she was breathing heavily, as if she had run the entire way.

"Richard! Oh my god, Richard, you're awake!" She lunged over his bed rail and threw her arms around him and hugged and kissed him.

"Are the kids coming?" he whispered.

"Yes, yes. They're on their way. What is it? Are you okay?" she asked.

"I'm fine, just fine, but I need to talk to you all." I went over to the bed and lowered the bedrail and told his wife, "Now you can get right up to him and snuggle him properly," which she did immediately.

Their two children arrived shortly after their mother. Connie was a young woman who favored her mother in appearance. She was without makeup and appeared exhausted yet excited just the same. She briskly walked into the room and exclaimed that she couldn't believe he was awake. She took off her coat and threw it over an empty chair and dropped her purse onto the seat. She leaned over the left side rail and hugged and kissed her father. Richard's son, Carl, arrived and hurriedly walked into the room. He took off his hat and was nearly identical in facial features as his father, but was much taller, and choked up as he hugged his father. They all gathered near the foot of his bed, awaiting Richard to tell them what was going on, exclaiming how happy they were that he was awake, and why did he want them there so quickly? He put up his right hand and beckoned his wife to approach. In a weak, slow, and steady voice, he said, "Claire, come here. I love you, dear, so very much. Thank you for taking such good care of me all these years." He reached up and wiped a tear streaming down her cheek. She was puzzled and asked him, "Richard, honey, what is all this about? What is going on?" Leaning her head on his hand, she sat next to him on the bed and pulled her knee up to better balance herself.

"Dear, it's time for me to go. Mom and Dad are here," he said, pointing to the left side of the room near the window. "And they're telling me that it's time. I asked them to please let me tell you good-bye, and they said okay." He spoke gently as a smile slowly grew on his face.

"What!? No, no! You can't go yet. Please, Richard, tell them not now!" She broke down onto his chest, wrapping her arms around him.

"Don't cry, dear . . . It's just my time." He leaned his head onto hers and embraced her for a long time, stroking her hair and patting her back. He held onto her as she sobbed, soaking his gown with her abundant tears. Claire fumbled with her tissue and blew her nose.

"Connie, come here," he said as he looked over at his daughter.

His wife slowly pulled herself up from his chest, grabbed another tissue, and backed away, giving Connie room to approach. "No, Daddy, no. Please don't . . ." she said as she slowly crept into his embrace.

Softly, tenderly, he told her, "You've been the joy of my heart, my little angel, and I love you so much. You take good care of my grandbabies now, won't you? Don't let them forget their Grandpa."

"Daddy, no, not yet. I'm sorry, I'm sorry," she sobbed.

"There is no need for being sorry, it's okay. I will never stop loving you." Connie had turned her head up toward his face, her head still resting on his chest. He put his frail hand on her cheek, patting her gently and wiping the tear that began trickling from her eye. Then he whispered, "It's all right, honey, you'll be okay." Then he kissed his finger and touched her lips. Connie slowly pulled away, silently sobbing, wiping her tears and blowing her nose.

"Carl, come here, son," he said, reaching out his arms to embrace Carl. Carl slowly and reluctantly approached his father's bed, as if this delay would prolong their time together. Carl leaned over the bed and hugged his father, resting his head on his father's heart. Richard slowly said, "My boy . . . my beautiful boy . . . I love you so much. But now, listen to me, Carl, you will be strong now, won't you? Take good care of your mother for me, okay? I'm counting on you to do that, do you understand? And you make sure that you tell Jimmy I'll be standing right with him at graduation, okay? Tell him that!" he said as he stroked his son's hair and embraced him as best he could. Carl nodded his head and sobbed after each statement and request. Carl straightened up, wiped his face and retreated from the bed. Claire returned to her husband's side and asked if there was any way to ask for more time, but Richard reassured her that he had already been given extra time, and that time was right now. This was a gift given to them, the gift of a final farewell.

Around forty-five minutes later, Richard became much weaker and sleepy. Twenty minutes later, he closed his eyes and slipped back into a coma with his family surrounding him, grieving quietly. Within the hour, the seventh floor phoned and said they had a private room available. We transferred Richard up to the floor at midnight, accompanied by his family. I settled them into the new, more spacious room, said good-bye to them, told them I would be praying for them, and closed the door behind me. I stopped by the nurses' station and asked the nurse who would be on duty the whole night to please call me at my extension should Richard pass during the night. I received a call from the nurse telling me that Richard passed peacefully at 2:06 AM.

Jacob: A Neglectful Child

We received a call from the ER one hot summer evening reporting a new admission. Jennifer took the report, and when she hung up the phone, she announced, "We've got a real train wreck coming up. You're not going to believe this one."

We set up the room and prepared it for a central line and possible intubation as the patient about to arrive was not doing well. We hurriedly spiked IV bags and attached them to the pumps awaiting his arrival. Jennifer walked to the supply room and came back with protective gowns, caps, masks, and shoe covers. As she handed them out to me and another nurse, she said, "We're going to need these because there's critters involved." So we began gowning up over our scrubs. Minutes later, the patient arrived, and the smell quickly filled the room. This poor man was brought in by ambulance after his neighbor, Bill, who had been watering his garden, heard Jacob calling out and crying. Bill went over and knocked on the door and was met by Jacob's daughter and her boyfriend. When Bill inquired about Jacob, he was told, "Mind your own damn business," and the door was forcefully slammed in his face. He stood outside the window listening to Jacob and decided to phone the police. The police arrived and, from the porch, heard Jacob wailing in the background. Jacob was removed from the home and brought to our hospital. Jacob's condition when he arrived was nothing short of appalling. He was a very thin man, riddled with lice, and hadn't been bathed in what appeared to be months. According to the police and ER report, he was kept in a back room of the home without air-conditioning or heat, and completely neglected. He had suffered a stroke the year before and was bedbound. His daughter moved in and promised to help him recuperate, but neglected to ever come through on her promise to actually care for him. No physical therapy was ever given to this poor man, and he lay in his bed day in and day out. The daughter, keeping his money and overtaking his home, afforded him no luxuries; in fact, it was obvious that the bare necessities of life were often denied him. Too cheap to buy incontinence pads or diapers for Jacob, she instead took a large drawstring trash bag, and poked holes in the bottom corners of the bag for Jacob's legs to fit through. She pulled up the bag around his waist and tightened the drawstring, making a makeshift diaper. Jacob lay in his own urine and excrement hour upon hour. His skin from the waist to the knees was excoriated, and he had huge bedsores on his sacrum and two large ones on the protruding bones of each hip. He also had large wounds on both heels and ankles covered in black eschar, a thick layer of dead skin. Large areas of open skin were found on the protruding bones of both scapulas on his upper back. The sacral and hip wounds were deep to the bone and were filled with maggots. There were so many maggots that it looked like one quivering, pulsating wound as hundreds upon hundreds of them crawled over each other. You could hear the faint *chk-chk-chk* sound they made as they wiggled around, eating the infected and necrotic portions of his gaping wounds. All of us gasped in horror, then Jennifer called out an order, "Come on, guys, help me get these critters off of him."

She grabbed a basin and a squirt bottle, filled it full with saline, and started cleaning the wounds out. We poured a bottle of rubbing alcohol into the suction canister on the wall, hooked up a suction tube, and sucked out as many as we could. It took three of us over three hours to clean Jacob's wounds and remove the maggots, pack the cleaned wounds with dressings, and cover them. Another nurse and I had to leave the room several times, overcome by the site of so many maggots, gagging from the smell. We added a few drops of peppermint oil to the inside of our masks to help the smell, but Jennifer didn't flinch as bugs and odors have never bothered her. The rest of us hated bugs, especially maggots! After dressing his bedsores, we soaked and scrubbed his hands and feet in a joint effort to clean and bathe him. We had to use large nail nippers in order to trim his nails, which were so overgrown they had curled over the ends of his fingers and toes. The nails caused scratches and wounds to the palms of his hands and the bottom portion of his toes. Little by little, we washed away the filth that covered him, and treated the lice that scurried through his hair, over his body, and onto the pillows and sheets. He was silent, moaning intermittently if we touched an area that was particularly raw and painful. His eyes were gentle and calm, and they thanked us with every gaze. His face bore witness to his suffering, and yet displayed a peaceful resignation.

"God bless you," he whispered. "Thank you." His expression became furrowed, and tears filled his eyes as he began to cry softly.

"Oh, Jacob, it's okay. We'll take good care of you," I said as I stroked the side of his cheek, then smoothed the hair near his temple. He slowly reached up, his hand shaking as he put his hand on my arm and weakly squeezed.

"Thank you," he whispered again.

As gently as we could, we cleaned every inch of him because he was completely filthy. We removed his dentures that were caked with rancid, dried, and rotting food. We rinsed his mouth and watched as he spit blackish-brown fluid into the basin. When his mouth was clean and fresh, we put his cleaned and scoured dentures back into his mouth, surprised that his mouth wasn't also covered in sores.

Adult Protective Services had been notified by the police during Jacob's transport to the ER, and their representative had accompanied Jacob into our CICU and photographed Jacob's body before, during, and after the cleaning. Statements were taken from the physicians, medical residents, and nurses who were assigned to his care. Two police officers remained in the unit; one speaking with the attending physicians and medical residents, while the other stationed himself on a chair outside of Jacob's room. Jacob's daughter, Yvonne, arrived two hours after we finished cleaning him and was very angry. She was allowed to come in and see her father for a short time, but the police officer stationed outside of Jacob's room informed her that the door would remain ajar. She entered his room and assaulted the staff with angry demands, never once speaking to her father.

"When was the last time you turned him? Why hasn't he been fed yet? He looks like he's in pain! If he dies, I will sue every single one of you! Whom do I have to speak to around here to get him adequately taken care of?" she snapped.

Listening outside within an earshot was his nurse, Jennifer. She walked into the room and explained to Yvonne what had been done. Yvonne glared down her nose at Jennifer and continued her barrage of demands. Jennifer, who stands only five feet two inches, stood her ground and finally snapped back, saying, "Your father has been neglected for a very long time, and I'm not talking a day or two. The condition that we found him in was not only appalling, but a direct result of months and months of neglect." She slowly inched toward Yvonne. "Instead of screaming your demands at us, what the hell have you been doing while he was under your care?" She edged closer to Yvonne, who took a few steps backward until she bumped into the corner of the room. The police officer stood in the doorway, watching intently. "Or would you like to see the pictures instead? Since you obviously haven't looked under that Hefty bag you so diligently tied around him, here! Maybe you'd like to see what we found? Want to see close-ups of maggots?" With that last statement, she jutted a handful of photographs toward her. As Jennifer was waving the photographs in her face, Yvonne stormed out of the room. The police officer met Yvonne at the door, said something to her, and then escorted her out of the unit. We never saw her again.

Jacob stayed in our unit for the next week, but he quickly declined. With every dressing change, another maggot would be found deep within the wound and would be removed. He soon became septic, as we all anticipated once the maggots were removed. And yet, despite IV antibiotics, the infection overtook him. He went into respiratory failure, was intubated and placed on the ventilator.

Septic shock soon followed, but he was so compromised from mal-nutrition and neglect that his poor body just couldn't hold on. Jacob died on a Friday night at 11:30.

Yvonne never again came into the unit. Within ten months of his death, several nurses received a summons from the county and had to give depositions regarding his case. There was overwhelming evidence against Yvonne, and as a result, it never went to court. Yvonne settled and was charged with negligent homicide. To all of us who were first-hand witnesses to the death of this poor man, it was a relief that she was held responsible for the reprehensible treatment she inflicted upon her own father.

Simon: A Glimpse of Heaven

The overhead paging system sounded, and we heard the operator say, "Code Blue, Emergency Room! Code Blue, Emergency Room!" Two hours later, I took report from the cardiac cath lab nurse and Simon was transferred to our unit, unconscious and on a ventilator. Once I made sure he was stabilized, I went out to the waiting room in search of his wife. I found Annie in the waiting room slowly pacing back and forth. Annie was a petite woman, neatly dressed in a long navy skirt with a white button-up blouse, clasped with a beautiful broach. A multicolored hand-knitted sweater was draped over her shoulders. Her hands were wringing a small worn hand-embroidered handkerchief, and a worn pocketbook was held securely in the bend of her elbow. Her hair was neatly pulled back in a small bun at the nape of her neck, and two haircombs held her hair neatly from her face. Her eyes met mine and were full of worry when she asked, "Is he okay? Is he awake?"

"He's doing okay, but right now, he isn't awake because we have him medicated to keep him calm and sedate while his heart recovers a bit. He's on the breathing machine and hooked up to IVs and the heart monitor. He also has his arms restrained because sometimes when people wake up on the breathing machine, their first instinct is to pull the tubes out of their mouths, and we don't want that to happen until he's a bit stronger." I reached over and put my arm around her, giving her a reassuring squeeze, and guided her into the unit and toward his room.

"It all happened so fast. He never said he had chest pain, just indigestion," she said nervously, and then proceeded to tell me what happened that night, including what she fixed him for dinner, the 911 call, the paramedics' arrival, and how, in her distress, she got lost on the way to the hospital. I led her into Simon's cubicle, answered her many questions, and explained each of the tubes, medications, and his expected course of treatment.

"I can't stay because I don't see well at night and driving is difficult for me. May I come back tomorrow?"

"Any time you want to come in, you are more than welcome. Here's the phone number that will dial directly into our unit. I'm here until seven thirty in the morning, so if you wake up in the middle of the night and want to check on him, just call me."

"Take good care of him, won't you?" she asked as she opened her arms to hug me.

"Yes, ma'am, I will, just like I would my own father." I hugged her back, and she left for the night.

Simon was a sixty-four-year-old soon-to-be-retired professor of economics at a nearby university. He was a tall large-bellied man with medium-brown skin splattered with freckles. His short-cropped hair, slightly receding, was a distinguished salt-and-pepper color. His hands were large, with very long neatly manicured fingers. The only jewelry he had was one silver wedding band that was covered in fine scratches from many years of wear. During the night, Simon continued to do well, and although unconscious, I told him my name and explained that I was his nurse and told him everything I was going to do to him before I did it. I explained that he had suffered a heart attack, and reassured him that he was doing just fine. I told him that, in the morning, we would remove his tubes, and he would be able to talk to us. His vital signs remained stable, and his sedation medication was also weaned incrementally in anticipation of extubation (the removal of the breathing tube and ventilator). When I returned to work that night and took report from the day-shift nurse, I was told that he was successfully extubated and off the ventilator. Since then, the nurse explained, he had been very emotional, intermittently crying, but unwilling to divulge to anyone the reason why. We were thinking it may have been a side effect of the sedation medications or the trauma of the resuscitation or any number of reasons. I went into his room to introduce myself and begin my shift.

"Hello, Simon, my name is—"

"I know who you are, Kelley. You took care of me last night when my wife was here."

"Yes, I did. How did you—you were unconscious, how did you know that? Did you hear me when I was talking to you?"

"Yes," he replied, then he bowed his head as tears flowed down his face.

"Honey, what's the matter? Why are you crying?" I took his hand and handed him a tissue, which he pressed onto his face. He heaved heavily through the tissue, then after wiping his face, he folded it neatly in four and wiped his eyes again. Then he said, "I can't believe this is happening."

I began to explain what happened to him last night when he interrupted me, "I know exactly what happened, my dear, you don't need to explain it to me."

Reluctant to disclose any further information, Simon spent the rest of the evening quietly recollected and occasionally teary. Throughout the shift, we related well to each other, and I was able to get him to smile now and again. Simon was an intelligent, humble man, and he often talked about God and about things going on in the world as different local and world news events flashed on the TV. He spoke about his love of music and was a very accomplished violinist. We compared our favorite classical composers, and he shared his regret of not pursuing a secondary degree in music. He spoke of his childhood, his marriage, and his work at the university. He and Annie had no children, but suffered two twenty-week miscarriages early in their marriage. He talked of his charity work as he volunteered frequently at one of the local soup kitchens. He expressed a deep empathy for those in need, a virtue that had been fostered by his parents when he was a young boy. His father was a lawyer, and his mother, a homemaker. They often brought homeless people into their home for a shower and a meal. They furnished them with new shoes, new clothes, heavy blankets or a coat during the winter, and loaded them with a sack of food and a few dollars for their pocket.

"They were always bringing some stranger home. It was not unusual to find one or more new faces sitting at the table or asleep in the spare room when we got home from school. In our home, no one was ever turned away if they were in need." His mother had died of breast cancer while in her early forties, and his father of a massive heart attack eleven months later. Although Simon was in college at that time, he said that their lives had much more of an impact on him, so much more than their deaths.

"When you love God as they did, and you are amenable to His will, death is viewed as that stepping stone into eternal life with God. They both had an unshakable faith and subsequently had no real fear of death."

He related that having grown up with parents like that, their generosity toward others became engrained in him. He frequently walked the streets, handing out food that Annie had made and packed up, as well as clothing and blankets, to the homeless. He was a very kind man, well-mannered, and always appreciative of every-thing we did for him.

At seven thirty in the morning, when my shift ended, I went into his room to say good-bye. "I'll be back tonight, Simon, and you and I are going to have another talk okay?"

"About what?"

"About the tears. What is it that makes you so sad?" I leaned forward and rested my elbows on his side rail.

"You'll never believe me," he sighed.

"You'd be surprised, Simon. In over twenty-five years of ICU nursing, I've heard and seen about everything imaginable. I really doubt that you could shock me."

We talked for a few more minutes, and after some prodding, he promised to tell me all about it when I returned that night.

47

"I'm going to hold you to it, okay?" I said to him as I squeezed his hand. Simon smiled softly, looked up at me, and said, "You're a persistent creature, aren't you? I think I'll call you Nurse Ratchet." A big smile grew on his face, and I felt like I had forged a new friendship.

When I returned that evening, our census was low, and the hospital overall was quiet. I quickly finished my initial duties, and then went in to see Simon. After assessing him and giving him his medications, I closed the glass doors in front of his cubicle, pulled up a chair, and lowered the side rail.

"Well, Nurse Ratchet, I suppose my interrogation is about to begin?" He smiled and fumbled for the button to raise the head of his bed higher. "I guess you won't be happy until I bare my soul, will you? But," he said, shaking his finger at me, "don't assume after hearing this that my next course of treatment includes four burly men in crisp white coats holding a straight jacket." He reached over and took a sip of water. Placing the cup back on his nightstand, he sat quietly for a time, and then began.

"After dinner, my stomach became very upset. I felt a terrible pressure in my lower chest, very similar to indigestion, so I went into the kitchen to get my antacids. The pressure and squeezing in my chest got worse and worse. I grabbed onto the counter as I began getting dizzy and was sweating profusely, and well, my legs just gave out on me, and I collapsed onto the kitchen floor. I remember looking up at the ceiling fan, thinking, *This is it, I'm going to die.* I heard Annie frantically speaking with the 911 operator as the room began to spin and then everything went black. I woke up to find myself up near the ceiling, looking down on my body lying on the floor. I watched Annie shaking me and crying, and I saw the paramedics arrive and begin working on me. I watched them put me onto a stretcher and wheel me to the ambulance. I watched from above the ambulance as it sped away, and I followed it for a time, hovering about thirty feet above it. But when the ambulance turned left onto Wilkens Avenue, I kept going straight. When I looked down, I recognized the houses and streets. I saw streetlights changing and traffic begin and stop." Simon looked over at me and said, "And when I looked down at myself"—he raised his hands up in front of him, fingers unfolded—"it didn't look like my regular body. I mean, it had form, but not exactly like normal skin and bones." He put his hands by his side and dropped his head back on his pillow. Still looking at me, he continued, "It's so very difficult to explain, and I can't seem to find the words for any of it."

"That's understandable, Simon, most people who try to explain this kind of experience to others are at a loss for words. Our vocabulary is incapable of describing the indescribable."

"So you've heard this kind of thing before?" he said, raising his head off the pillow. He appeared not only surprised but also relieved.

"Oh, yes, many times."

After a slight pause, Simon continued, "Well, I kept going at a steady pace and was now as high as the tops of the telephone poles. Everything was so quiet, but when I travelled over areas of trees, I could hear birds chirping and leaves rustling. When over the reservoir, I could hear lapping water, frogs croaking, and crickets chirping. When I was above the city, cars honking and people talking. Gradually, I lifted higher and higher and then escalated at such an incredible speed that I wondered why I wasn't burning up. But even at this speed, I felt no pain, no heat or discomfort, and no wind, only a light soothing breeze. I flew out of our atmosphere and into space, and yet in the vacuous silence of space, I heard the most beautiful music. It was a music I was unfamiliar with, and it was so incredibly beautiful, beyond any composer I had ever heard. I slowed down and turned around and looked at the earth." He raised his hands in front of him with his palms up, as if cupping something. "There it was— just hanging there, suspended and surrounded by nothing. It was so immense in the middle of the blackness of space, and I was surprised at the sheer enormity of it. I wondered how these huge and awesome planets are suspended. How does something of such incredible weight just hang there, supported by nothing?" Simon paused and turned toward me. "You understand that I had no control over what was happening to me. I had no input over where I went or what was shown to me, and yet I had no fear. I just accepted and was open to it all. I slowly turned away from the earth and quickly escalated to a speed that I knew was very near or surpassed the speed of light. So as

I went, I shot past stars and planets, slowing down several times near a particular planet, as if God were allowing me to take in the beauty of His creation. I saw planets that were completely unknown to us, and when I slowed down and drew near them, I again heard the most delicate music. I intuitively learned that what I was hearing was the music of that particular planet. Each one was different but beautifully composed, ethereal in nature, and by instruments that only vaguely resembled in sound our string instruments, but very similar too to the woodwinds, like oboes and clarinets. In the background, still in perfect harmony, the tinkling of bells shimmered in and out. The crescendo and decrescendo of these 'instruments' overlapped, and each one, in turn, took over a melody. Very much like our counterpoint compositions, you know, like Palestrina. Are you familiar with that style of music?" he asked, raising his eyebrows and looking at me over his glasses.

"I am familiar with Palestrina, his compositions were truly inspired."

"Everything that I heard and saw was so completely perfect in its design and composition that I was awestruck. You see, I learned that everything God has created sings to Him—all of the planets, the stars, every single galaxy—filling the universe with an immense orchestra of praise. It's so incredibly beautiful! I wasn't surprised at the music, only by its incomparable loveliness."

He smiled, looked down at his fingers all the while fiddling with the tissue. He lifted his eyes toward the cupboard near the foot of his bed and continued. "When I looked at these beautiful galaxies, the design of each one of them was just breathtaking. Each was so different from the other that they resembled nothing I have ever seen from Hubble telescope photographs. Yet even in the darkness of space, there shines so vividly such beauty that it inspired me to sing out praise to God. I began singing out loud, singing to Him how much I loved Him. As I sang, the music that I heard in the background harmonized perfectly with the melody that sprang from my lips. It was just incredible, and it fit and flowed so perfectly." He smiled, still gazing toward the end of the bed, and then looking down at his lap, he continued, "I sped up faster and faster, and found myself completely encased in darkness and propelling toward what I thought was a very large star in the distance. As I came closer, the light of the star grew brighter and brighter, surrounding me more and more until there wasn't any space left, and I was completely enveloped in this light. Now, it's not as if something was pushing me into this light, you see, but I felt drawn into it, as if my soul were magnetically pulled toward it. And the closer I came toward it, the more my desire to reach it intensified." He dropped his head and sighed. "I found myself in a room completely made of light from floor to ceiling, and then my mother and father appeared. They were young, very happy, and we were so excited to see each other again. I couldn't believe how much love flowed between us and how thrilled and happy we were to be in each other's company again. My father took me by the hand and led me into a huge, rolling meadow. Leaving the lighted room was like stepping out of a huge soap bubble. That thin membrane, no thicker than that of a soap bubble, was the only thing that separated these two areas. When we stepped from the room of light and entered into this separate world, I knew instinctively that I was on the outskirts of heaven. The breeze was warm and was very much alive. Every time it brushed up against me, it brought with it such an incredible feeling of happiness and peace. The place where we were standing was immense and so beautiful—it was somewhat like the scenery or landscape that we have here on earth, but so much more beautiful, just indescribable. There were trees of species I have never seen before and beautiful beyond words, all in different sizes, and many were just enormous. There were flowers, lakes, and rivers, but on a scale that was incomparable to earthly size and beautiful beyond words and in colors that don't exist here on earth, filling everything with incredible beauty. And the music—oh, the music! It just permeated everything and yet originated from everything. Yes, everything in heaven seemed to create its own music, and yet it all melted together into such a perfect harmony. I have never heard a melody on earth that compares. These harmonies blended back and forth, up and down, in and out with such incredible beauty that it overwhelmed my soul. It was alive, if you can imagine that, and it passed through me and filled me up, quenching every desire, and I knew that I was home.

"As I looked in absolute amazement at the breathtaking beauty that surrounded me, my mother came up from behind and turned me to the right, and there directly in front of me . . ." Simon's chin quivered, and with a voice stifled with emotion, he said, "Right there, standing in front of me, was Jesus." Wiping the tears away, he fiddled with the tissue in his hands, blew his nose, and continued, "I couldn't believe it was my Lord, my Savior. Jesus opened up His arms, and beaming from the holes in His hands and feet and side were rays of beautiful pulsating light that were so welcoming that I flew into His arms so hard I should have knocked Him over." Simon sighed and smiled up at me. "Those feelings that I had before, thinking I was complete, paled in comparison to what overwhelmed me in His embrace. Every molecule of my soul was exhilarated beyond human imagination. Every wave of love that poured out of Him flew into every tiny, minute recess of my soul to the point that I felt like I would explode should it continue. Love, forgiveness, acceptance pulsated into me, and I was left with a complete and perfect knowledge and understanding of myself. Every fault and failing filled me with such remorse that I fell on my knees at His feet. I clung to His feet and kissed His wounds as He continued to fill my soul, wave after wave of ever-increasing love. It was such tender and compassionate love that I had to beg Him to stop." Simon wiped his copious tears and struggled to keep back the sobs straining to the surface. "How could I have ever offended such a God?" Simon paused, pressing the tissue to his eyes, and then removing the tissue, he folded it in half. "Jesus reached down, took me by the hands and stood me up in front of Him. He looked at me, through me, and then smiled, and immediately I was completely cleansed. All of my sins, my failures, my inability to be patient, loving, and caring—all of my unworthiness and every stain of sin were completely gone."

Simon stopped and inhaled abruptly; he wiped his eyes and blew his nose. After a pause to collect himself, he continued. "'Come,' He said, 'I want you to see.' We were then immediately standing on the outskirts of an immense city that pulsated and sparkled with light. This light that fills heaven is so incredibly bright, but it never burdens the senses. You know how your eyes react when you go outside on a bright day and they strain to cover themselves from its glare? The light of heaven surpasses millions of times that of our sun, and yet my eyes were never offended in the least. I could easily look at it and see everything without the slightest discomfort, and everything was filled with this light. There were no shadows anywhere." Simon was looking up at the clock hanging on the wall, as if visualizing again the wonder that his eyes only a short time ago had enjoyed. He shook his head as if to get himself back on track, diverted his eyes down toward his fingers fumbling with the tissue. "We were standing on a tall hilltop covered with the most luscious foliage and flowers that I have ever seen. Where we were standing looked down on a beautiful road that led into this city, when suddenly, we were surrounded by people. I instantly knew who they were, although many I had forgotten about on earth. They were all cheering and welcoming me so joyously. Each and every one of them hugged me, and there were so many of them! I saw neighbors and friends, my brother and sister, a man I gave a $20 bill to on the street, and countless more. I saw a man I had come across on the street in the dead of winter who was too weak to move. I covered him with a blanket, and he was burning with fever, frostbitten, and wreaked of the streets. I offered him hot coffee, but he was too weak to take even a small sip. I called EMS and stayed with him, holding him in my arms while we waited. He asked me to pray with him, so we prayed the Lord's Prayer—but he died in my arms before the ambulance arrived. I had often thought of him, and there he was, radiantly beautiful and perfectly whole. Then out from the center of this crowd emerged a young man and a young woman, and I knew immediately they were my children." Simon glanced over at me and smiled, and straightening the sheet on his lap, he continued. "Here they were, fully-grown and were full of such beauty that I have never seen any human being so beautiful in all my life. I immediately knew why they had died and how they had prayed for Annie and me from the moment they entered heaven. I threw my arms around them and hugged them, and after all of these years of being childless, I was at last a father! It was the best and the happiest of reunions." He beamed a smile up at me, tears glistening in his eyes. "We spoke for a time, and then they all said good-bye and disappeared. Jesus looked at me, and His expression was so excited and joyful. He placed his arm around my shoulder and said, 'I want you to see what I have prepared for you from the moment you were created.'" Simon broke down and sobbed, and leaning forward, he wrapped his hands over his face and wept. After a minute or so, he straightened up and wiped his eyes. "Had I any idea what was waiting for me, and how much my Lord truly loved me"—he looked up and pointed his finger at me—"I never would have let you people bring me back!"

After a long time of silent tears, and a few more tissues, he lifted his head and went on. "We were standing before a huge structure similar to our buildings, but not made from stone or brick because you could see through it. It was incredibly beautiful and shone as bright as the sun. This . . . this was my mansion!" (Then Simon quoted the biblical passage in John 14:2, "In my Father's house, there are many mansions . . ." and Matthew 6:20–21, "Lay up for yourselves treasures in Heaven, where neither moth nor rust destroys and where thieves do not break in and steal . . .") "But as I stood in front of it and looked into this immense structure, it was revealed to me that my life was the architect and the source of its construction and design. Everything that I had done during my life that was good, kind, and directed toward the good of another human being, it was all there. Every bowl of soup, every piece of bread, every blanket or an encouraging word, every tender gesture done for the love of God built and engineered it all. He rewarded to the nth degree every single thing I had done here on earth that pleased Him. I didn't deserve any of it, to be brutally honest, but His generosity magnified my feeble efforts on earth to such a degree that I was awestruck standing before such incredible magnificence. It was beyond anything any mortal mind could remotely comprehend, and it was specific only to me. No other structure looked like mine because every soul's life experience is unique. Your life, your gifts and graces, are different than mine and vice versa. All of my prayers, every single one that I had ever offered up to heaven were there. Prayers of praise, thanksgiving, and petition were there, and all of them in combination formed the mortar that held it all together, adorning it with such beauty that there is no way that I could begin to describe it. But the prayers that I had said for other people were the most pristine and the most ornate of its decoration. Oh, if only I had the words to tell you what it all looked like." He bowed his head and shook it slightly as if in disbelief. He adjusted himself in the bed, reached for the cup on the over-bed table, and took another drink.

"I stood there for some time trying to take it all in and kept repeating, 'Jesus, oh, my Jesus!' When I turned to the side and looked at Him, He had the most spectacular smile." Simon's voice broke again in a voice full of emotion he went on. "He was like a father surprising a child on his birthday. He beamed with such incredible happiness, like a father watching a child open a tremendous present. I felt immediately how pleased He was at everything I had done for Him during my life. He placed His arms around me and pulled me close to Him and into my soul I heard Him say, 'I love you!' I melted in His embrace and was so overwhelmed with love for Him that my soul rejoiced in complete and utter praise. Incredible, spontaneous adoration sprang from my heart, so much so that I could have easily praised and adored Him for all eternity. It was all so overwhelming and exhilarating that there are simply no words to express what overtook my heart in His embrace and in His presence. The love that emanates from Him is simply indescribable and so complete that nothing, absolutely nothing, in my life that I have ever experienced comes remotely close to it. Despite feeling so immensely overwhelmed, I was absolutely and completely happy, for nothing was lacking while I was there. You know, my wife, all my friends, my home, and everything I worked for here in this life? None of it mattered. I was completely at ease in leaving it all behind without even looking back. And my Annie, whom I love more than anyone, I was completely content to leave her behind because I was finally home, and I was absolutely fulfilled and completely happy . . . completely happy."

Simon paused, dropped his head back onto his pillow, then turned his head and looked over at the window. After a time of silence, he continued, "Ah . . . but then the worst moment came." He reached over and placed his cup back on the table. He laid his head back on the pillow and looked up toward the ceiling. "That dreadful, awful moment when Jesus put His hand on my shoulder and told me that I had to go back." He pulled his head up and looked down as he folded his hands together onto his lap. "I was crushed in my soul. I begged Him over and over to please let me stay, but He explained that it wasn't my time. 'Not yet, son, I have something more for you to do.'"

There was a long pause, and Simon readjusted his pillow. He took both hands and smoothed back the hair on his head. With a long emotional sigh, he grabbed another tissue and looked over at me. "Do you have any idea how difficult it is to be in His presence one minute and then thrust back into a body that is hooked up to machines?" He looked up past the monitor and IV poles to the window. "I felt like I'd lost everything." He stared out the window at the sunset as copious tears melt down his face. He looked back over at me, wiped his eyes again, and said, "It was so painful to leave Him that, in that very instant, I understood completely what hell would be like. I understood that to be without Him, even for a moment, was unbearable, but forever and ever? Oh yes, that's what hell is." He paused for a moment and then looked up at me with such a sad expression. "You know, when you are standing in front of Jesus, it is as if the entire universe was created specifically for you. Remember all of those planets and galaxies that I had passed by on my way to heaven? I felt as if all of them were made especially for me to enjoy the beautiful imagination and the creative power of my God. In His presence, Jesus makes you feel as though everything, everything He went through when He walked the earth—His life, His death, the enormity of His wounds—it was all done *just for you*, and He would willingly do it again if it meant that you could be with Him for all eternity. When He looks into your eyes, He sees everything. There is nothing hidden from those beautiful eyes, and yet you don't feel fear, or at least I didn't. He makes you feel that you are the only one in the universe, so great is His love for you!" He reached over and patted my hand. "When Jesus told me I had to leave, I knew deep down in the depths of my soul that it was the right thing for me, but still," he shrugged, "I had to at least try." He smiled and continued,

"I don't know when I will see Him again, but I do know that when my body gives out, I don't ever want to be stopped from going home to heaven."

"Tell me, Simon, what did Jesus look like?"

"He was incredible! He radiated incredible love, holiness, and absolute and perfect purity. But above all, He exudes such regal majesty that you are compelled to worship, to adore, and to love Him, as He is overwhelming and stunning in His magnificence and beauty. He is tall and completely and perfectly masculine and so wonderfully handsome. He had brown hair and the most engaging deep, beautiful eyes. I could have looked at Him and nothing else for all eternity, truly . . . for all of eternity. But He looks nothing like any artistic rendering I have ever seen on earth, as so many are almost effeminate looking. But He looked like you, like me, like that woman over there, that doctor there," he said as he pointed toward the nurses' station. "It is really very difficult to explain, but looking at you, I see Him. Looking at her over there and him over there, I see my Jesus. I see Him in everyone, and He's very much a part of everyone because we were created in His image you see. You know that's what He meant when He said, 'Whatsoever you do to the least of these, My brothers, you did it to Me.' Ah, yes—I see Him now in everyone, and it's so obvious to me now that I can't believe how blind I was before."

"Wow, Simon, what an incredible experience! I'm glad I coerced you into sharing it with me," I giggled at him.

"That you did, Nurse Ratchet, that you did." He smiled and squeezed my hand. Although I had so many questions I wanted to ask him, I could see that he was becoming tired. I helped Simon reposition himself on his side, tucked him in, and let him sleep. I heard him intermittently blowing his nose, staring out at the sunset through the window he faced. Two days later, Simon was weaned off his IV medications and transferred to our step-down unit, but he developed congestive heart failure. His heart was so weakened from the heart attack that he wasn't physically capable of returning to work. He required a permanent pacemaker and an internal defibrillator. He initially refused it, but the tears of Annie softened his heart. Simon stayed a total of two weeks in the hospital, and I often stopped by his room to talk to him before work or after work. He was always so happy to see me, and he frequently told me how he longed for heaven and how he prayed constantly.

We forged a wonderful friendship that continued even after he was discharged home. I was invited many times to stop by his home after work to visit him. He and Annie lived in a small modest rancher that was simple in its décor but always immaculately clean. There was a small table that seated four near a large kitchen window that looked out over his small neatly manicured lawn and Annie's extensive vegetable gardens. A birdbath and feeder were set outside the window that welcomed an array of local birds, which Simon said they both enjoyed watching. Annie always kept the feeders stocked, and I never saw the woman sit for long as she busied herself about the kitchen or out in her garden tending to her vegetables and flowers. When the kitchen windows were opened during the summer, the scent of lilacs and roses breezed into the kitchen.

During one of our visits, Simon talked about how he shared his experience with his wife, then his friends, and finally his church. "I may not be able to work anymore, but I can still talk. If people are willing to listen and change their lives because of my experience, if I can touch even just one soul, then I'm willing to keep talking. Then my work for God is successful."

One morning, I stopped by after work, and after our usual cup of coffee, I asked him a question that had me wondering since our first meeting. "Simon, may I ask you something?"

"Sure," he said as he lowered his cup to the table.

"What was that 'something more' that Jesus wanted you to do?"

Simon sighed and said, "What my Jesus put into my heart that day was the absolute realization that God doesn't desire that anyone go to hell. Since I've been back, I can't erase the feeling of urgency that has been seared into my heart and soul. Eternity is very, very, very long, you see, and for any soul to be lost, to be permanently separated from a God who loves them so much, causes me physical pain to even think about. The soul, the human soul, is His most beloved and the most beautiful of His creations, and each and every one is so very precious to Him. The realization that many souls don't really know Him or don't love Him and are lost to hell forever was the main reason for my tears. I have been unable to evict it from my thoughts since my return. My task, my 'something more to do,' is that I must pray constantly for sinners. For their conversion, for their salvation, and to keep them from hell, and that is my task until my Jesus calls me home. Remember my mansion? Remember that the most beautiful of decorations that made it so magnificent were prayers for other people? Any and all prayer for other people is so efficacious that one small prayer may be enough to change a hardened sinner into a repentant one. Nothing is wasted when it comes to prayer. It is our most beautiful and most powerful means to bend the ear of God, because to pray for others is a sacrifice. Even though it may not seem to be a sacrifice, we sacrifice our time, we put aside our own petitions even temporarily, and ask God to help someone else. And to save just one soul from being banished from the presence of God for all eternity? Well, that is all I think about, and it fills me with such dread and such anxiety that the tears just fall out of me, and so I pray constantly. I sleep very little because it fills every minute of my day and night. Hell, that horrible place, what an awful finality! I would have much preferred to stay in heaven than be left here with this anchor tied to my heart." He shook his head, staring down at his coffee cup. Then looking up at me, he nodded and said, "But it is a task that was asked of me directly from Jesus, a task that I agreed to and one that demands my full attention. I won't let Him down because whatever He wants is what I want. I long with every fiber of my being to be with Him again. When my time here is done and He calls me home for good, only then will my soul be content. You see, eternity is not long enough to adore and to thank such a wonderful God. Yes, a God that would rather die on a cross than be separated from us, can you imagine? That fact alone will take forever to thank Him."

Six months later, Annie arrived in our unit with a massive stroke. The entire right side of her brain was completely obliterated by a bleed. She arrived unconscious and on a ventilator. Simon never left her side, and we made arrangements for him to stay with her around the clock. He often stroked her hair and her face and told her,

"Wait until you see it, Annie, it's so beautiful. You go on ahead and save me a spot, I'll see you again very soon."

Annie died twenty-four hours after she arrived in our hospital. Simon cried when she died, but he said they were tears of joy. He bent over her body, kissed her forehead, and whispered, "Oh, Annie, I will miss you, but I know where you are. Hug my Jesus for me and ask Him to come for me soon."

Simon moved about a year after Annie died to the neighboring county. There, he could be closer to his sister and her children. I received a few letters, and we spoke on the phone now and again. He related how Annie had come to him in a dream and was surrounded by the most beautiful light. He said how he ached to leave this world and to be near Jesus again. The following year, I received a letter from his sister telling me that Simon died peacefully in his sleep on Christmas Eve.

The Inpatient Hospice Unit

My interview for hospice was promptly at 2:00 PM. This was a Catholic hospice that was supported by a large team of physicians and nurse practitioners, Catholic clergy as well as other denominations, nuns, social workers, and a huge team of hospice volunteers. It was a twenty-one-bed unit caring for a wide variety of patients with differing socioeconomic backgrounds and religious faiths. When I stepped off the elevator, I was amazed at how beautiful it was. At the end of the hallway, a large mosaic wall fountain stretched from the ceiling to the floor, bathing the background of glass stones with the soft murmur of trickling water. It was not only beautiful, but also quiet and peaceful. There were no alarms, no bells and buzzers, no ventilators screeching in the background. There was only silence with intermittent soft voices that were barely audible. When I walked toward the central desk, I was greeted by a tall robust woman with a smile as large as she was. She introduced herself as Helen, the unit's head nurse, and jutted out her hand to shake mine. She led me to the back offices and offered me a seat in front of her desk.

"So I was looking over your résumé. You've been an ICU nurse for a lot of years, and over twenty years at your current hospital, is that right?" She looked up from her papers and over her glasses at me, then shot me a quick smile.

"Yes, ma'am," I said nervously.

"That's a long time in one place. Are you leaving there for good, or are you planning on doing both jobs?" she asked as she shuffled the pages she held in her hands.

"Well, I was planning on doing both until I got a good feel for hospice. If it is what I am hoping it will be, I hope to leave the hospital and stay here full time," I said, fumbling with my purse, which then slipped out of my hand and spilled onto the floor.

"You nervous?" she giggled with a big smile on her face. I picked up my purse and put back the few items that tumbled from it.

"Ma'am, I haven't been on an interview in twenty-two years. You can't believe how nervous I am!" I smiled and giggled back.

"There's nothing to be nervous about, we're very laid-back here, just one big happy family. Tell me now, why did you want to become a nurse?"

"My father was a physician, and he used to tell us about his interesting patients, which usually happened around the dinner table. He started out in family practice, but then went into emergency medicine. One day, he cared for a boy who had been bitten by a rattlesnake. He brought home the film that they took of the actual snake. He said they took the X-ray 'just for fun—to see what it had for lunch.' Holding it up to the dining room light, you could see in the belly of the snake, the distinct skeleton of a rat. I was amazed as Dad pointed out the head, ribcage, and tail. I was in grade school at the time, but from that day on, I knew what I wanted to do when I grew up. I wanted to help people who were sick or injured."

"Interesting . . . Why do you want to be a hospice nurse after all these years of ICU? It seems like the complete opposite of what you're used to," she asked as she leaned back in her chair, tossing my résumé onto the desk in front of her.

"Truthfully, I am growing tired of shoving tubes into people with irreversible, irreparable disease processes with no hope for recovery. There is little to no dignity in their last moments here on earth when they are tied down in a bed, hooked up to every conceivable device to prolong the inevitable. Don't get me wrong, I believe these things are necessary and good in most situations, but in some cases, I don't feel right about it. Like I'm torturing people whose outcome will be death no matter what we do. My favorite patients are the DNR patients. I can spend time with them, facilitate their comfort, and help their families with their grief. It's when my focus isn't directed on heroic intervention that I feel I can do the most good, physically and spiritually." I smiled up at her and settled back into my chair and crossed my legs. "I've thought about becoming a hospice nurse for many years, and I feel certain that God is calling me to this type of nursing."

"Well, let me tell you how things go here because you will find that it is vastly different than what you've been used to in the hospital." She leaned forward, put her elbows onto the desk and folded her hands together. "We do vital signs twice a day," she said, and she looked over her bifocals to see my reaction.

"Twice a day?" I asked, almost dumfounded, since I was used to doing them every two hours at a minimum.

Helen laughed. "I thought you'd be surprised at that. We also don't do IV fluids, central lines, non-invasive mask ventilation, or anything else invasive. Many of our patients are cancer patients, and if they have a port, we will access it to give pain medications. We focus on the patient's comfort, whether it be physical or spiritual, or both. You see, dying involves a lot of work for the patient. Often times a significant amount of emotional or spiritual issues need to be reconciled before death can come. Our job is to ease their transition, to calm and alleviate physical symptoms so that this work of dying, this resolution of their life, can take place. The dying process is also very much an individualized one, and there are stages that each patient goes through. Now, I'm not talking about denial, anger, bargaining, etc., I'm talking about actual physical stages. These include sleeping more, the dwindling of the appetite, withdrawal from those around them, agitation, confusion, as well as a host of other changes. The confusion that we most often see here isn't really your typical confusion. The dying patient often lingers between two worlds, the physical and the spiritual. The confusion many times is associated with this lingering and movement spiritually in and out of these two worlds. As you will see, when they are working to resolve different aspects of their lives, they move back and forth from the present to the past. Do you see how this would be confusing? One minute you're in 1943 in the middle of a war, and the next you're lying in a bed in an unfamiliar place with no underwear on." She smiled, and I couldn't help but giggle at her description. "Our job here is to support them physically, emotionally and spiritually, as well as their families, until they move into their final phase, their eternal phase of life. We cater to their every need, but I need to reaffirm first and foremost that we are here to support them and ease their transition, not push them over the edge. We will help you to recognize the different stages, what treatments and medications will help, and how to help the families in the journey. I'm sure you'll catch on quickly."

"How do you administer pain medications if they don't have a port?"

"If they don't have a port, we use subcutaneous catheters. They're small catheters that resemble the butterflies you use to draw blood in the hospital. They are placed in the subcutaneous tissue of the arms or thighs. Occasionally, we put them on the posterior portion of the upper back too. They are changed out every ten days or sooner, should they become irritated." She looked up at me, waiting for a response.

"Every ten days? Subcutaneous? No more digging around trying to find a vein? That sounds good to me."

"Here at hospice, you will go from high-tech to high-touch. Think you can handle that?" She smiled and glanced up at me.

"Oh, yes, absolutely!"

"Come on, I'll show you around the place." She got up and led me out the door. At the end of the tour, I was sold on going to work there. When we went back into Helen's office, she asked, "So what do you think? Do you think you'd like to work here in hospice?"

"Please hire me!" I said in a playful begging tone.

Helen threw back her head and began to laugh. "Great! Let me call downstairs and set you up with the next orientation class. Welcome to the team!"

She stood up, shook my hand, and gave me a huge smile. I realized very soon after that it was the best decision I had made. For the first time, I felt I had found my niche, my true calling as a nurse.

Donald: I've Seen Jesus Before

Donald was a sixty-one-year-old male suffering from metastatic lung cancer. He initially had no symptoms except for pain in his back and tingling in his legs down to his feet. Thinking that it was due to his chronic disk problem, he ignored it until the pain and numbness became continual and very bothersome. He went to his doctor, who sent him for an MRI of his spine. When the results returned, there was a large mass noted in the upper left lung field. It also showed tumors around his thoracic spine pressing on the spinal cord; a very large tumor in his right lung; tumors on the adrenal glands, which sit on top of both kidneys; and large spots in his liver, which were more than suspicious. His PET scan showed that the extent of his diffuse metastasis had extended to the bones of his pelvis and left thigh as well. He was immediately sent to a leading oncologist in the city, who performed biopsies. The biopsies showed a very fast-growing cancer that appeared to have originated in his lung. After a series of chemotherapy and radiation treatments, it was found that his cancer did not respond well at all. Donald subsequently refused further treatments. After lengthy discussions, all physicians involved recommended hospice care.

He was brought into our unit early on a Thursday night. Jane, our nurse practitioner, met with Donald and his wife to discuss a treatment plan to help control his pain. She ascertained his desires and wishes regarding his care, and she reviewed what our hospice would provide. Donald asked what was normally seen and experienced by people with his diagnosis as death approached. Jane very gently began explaining different changes to be expected, when Donald's wife stood up and began to yell at her.

"This is bullshit! How dare you! Have you no sympathy at all? This whole hospice idea was done behind my back! It has been a conspiracy from the very beginning to keep me out of the loop." Then turning to her husband lying in the bed, she jutted a finger at him and yelled, "And you! You have done nothing for months! When you're gone, how am I supposed to live? What am I supposed to live on? Every day that you're lying in this bed is putting me further and further into debt! By the time all of this is done, I won't have a pot to piss in!" She turned on her heels and stormed out of the unit, mumbling under her breath. Jane followed her out the door and down the hallway. I looked over at Donald and could see he was exhausted and humiliated. Overwrought with emotion, he began to cry. He was trying to get the words out when I reached down and took his hand.

"I know you've been through a lot these past few months . . . It's okay, we'll take very good care of you."

Donald continued to cry, so I pulled up a chair and sat next to him. He proceeded to tell me that his wife was so angry at him, at the situation, and at God. He said he worried about her since he felt her faith was weak. He explained that his home was paid for and that he had paid his life insurance premiums six months in advance, which would leave her wanting for nothing as his policy exceeded $400,000. He couldn't understand why she couldn't understand this? He was so tired and so weak that he didn't have the strength to help her through her grief, and was so distraught at how she spoke to him. He looked at me and said, "I don't know what to do." He wiped his tears, repeating those last words.

"Donald, people handle grief in many ways. Anger is sometimes one of those ways." He nodded, silently sobbing. Thinking there might be more to the story, I asked him, "Donald, are you afraid of dying?"

He looked up and smiled. "No, I'm really not. Jesus is my Savior, and I can't wait to see Him again."

"See Him again? You've seen Him before?"

He nodded and then told me this story, "I worked for a company that designed and helped maintain large cranes. You know, the ones used to build skyscrapers, used on loading docks to unload overseas shipping vessels, oilrigs, etc. Anywhere where a crane was required, we designed and built them specifically to the needs of the clients. My job required that I travel extensively throughout the country. I was very successful and a complete workaholic, but I also had a big drinking problem. Back in 1985, some associates from my company flew to New York City and closed a huge deal. We all met back at the hotel for a celebratory dinner. The alcohol was flowing freely that night, and I didn't hold back. A woman from logistics, whom I had known for years, came over and gave me a hug, and she stayed nearby the rest of the night, openly flirting with me. Now, let me tell you, I was happily married. I had no reason whatsoever to wander, but I kept drinking and got very, very drunk. The next morning I woke up, not remembering much of the night before, but when I opened my eyes, I immediately sensed that there was someone else in the room with me. I slowly turned over on my back, just dreading to see if that woman was in my bed. When I turned my head, I was relieved that she wasn't there! But I'd become so inebriated the night before that I had no idea how I even got up into my room. I rolled over again on my side, happy that I was alone, but the feeling that someone was in my room was still there. Finally, I rolled over on my back and looked at the foot of my bed, and that's when I saw Him. I rubbed my eyes, thinking I was seeing things, but He was still there. Then He spoke, and His voice was a deep, majestic baritone, and he said, 'Do you know who I am?' 'Yes, Lord, I do,' I answered, and He looked at me with an expression of disappointment and sadness. Then He said, 'I saved you from something last night that would have ruined you, your marriage, and your life. I will not do it again.'

I nodded my head, and He disappeared. From that day on I never had another drink."

"Were you frightened to be in the presence of Jesus?" I asked.

"At first I was, but I was more humiliated knowing how drunk I had been only a few hours earlier. But the expression on His face struck me to the core. He was so sad, so disappointed in me, but you know, at the same time, I was immediately overcome by such an incredible love that flowed from Him that I was completely amazed by it. It is really difficult to even attempt to describe it, but He was just standing there, disappointed, but still loving me. It was a love that you could feel, physically feel. I knew that I could embrace and accept it, or I could refuse and reject it. Even in my embarrassment I grabbed onto it and embraced it. His love was so strong, so forgiving, and it flowed over me like a heartbeat." Donald made a fist with his right hand and put it up to his chest, thumping it onto his heart. "*Boom-boom-boom*. I wanted to die right then and there just to have that forever. It is like nothing I have ever experienced before, and from that day on, I never touched booze again. I never wanted to disappoint Him ever again. And you know, since then, I have no real fear of death at all, because when I remember Him and remember how much He loves me, I am anxious to be in His presence again. I'm looking forward to it with all my heart. I was relieved when I was diagnosed because I know that soon I will be with Him again."

We talked a little bit more, but I saw he was getting tired, so I tucked him in and left the room. His wife never returned, so I checked on him throughout the night, and he slept peacefully. Around five in the morning, I went back into his room to give him his medication and offered to bathe him. He asked if there was any way he could have a shower, so I grabbed my nursing assistant, and we helped him onto a shower chair, put extension tubing onto his nasal cannula oxygen, and wheeled him into the shower. We soaped him up well, and you could tell he relished the warm water as we rinsed the shampoo and the bubbles away. We quickly dried him, dressed him in fresh pajamas, combed his hair, rolled him back over to the bed, and sat him back on his bed dressed with fresh linens. He sat at the edge of the bed, quite winded from that little bit of exertion. I heard audible wheezing, so I upped his oxygen a bit and gave him a nebulizer treatment. I sat with him, as he was anxious about not catching his breath right away. I talked him through it, reassuring him that his breathing would calm down. I explained that given his compromised lungs, even the slightest exertion would cause him to become short of breath, but that it would ease up. When the treatment finished, I removed the mask from his face. He reached up and took my hand and said, "I haven't had a bath since I left the hospital three weeks ago. I can't tell you how inhuman a man feels when he isn't cared for. Look at my face! I haven't had a shave since the hospital, and it isn't like me to be unshaven."

"I thought you normally wore a beard! I'm so sorry. Do you want me to shave you now? Are you up to it?"

He smiled and nodded his head. "Please?"

I trimmed his beard, lathered up his face and shaved him, and brushed his teeth. When that was finished, I lifted his legs into the bed and pulled the covers up to his chest. He grabbed my hands and said, "Are you going home soon?"

"Yes, Donald, my shift ends in about an hour."

"I have been blessed to have you care for me tonight, thank you." He smiled and squeezed my hands.

"No, Donald, it was my privilege to care for you, I'll see you Monday."

That Monday I entered Donald's room to begin his assessment. He had declined drastically since his admission and was very lethargic. Since he was peaceful and without signs of pain or struggle, I continued down the hall and assessed the rest of my patients. Around midnight, I had a feeling that I should go into Donald's room and check on him (I learned very early on in my nursing career not to ignore those feelings). When I entered Donald's room, he was lying on his back with his eyes opened and staring at the ceiling. I turned up the dimmer switch a little to get a better view of him. As I approached his bed, his lips were moving almost imperceptibly, but his eyes were transfixed on something on the ceiling. I reached over and touched his arm. He slowly turned his head and looked over at me and smiled slightly, then he turned his head back toward the ceiling.

"Donald, what do you see?" I asked, gently caressing his shoulder. I leaned in closely to see if I could make out what he was saying when I heard him softly whisper, "Jesus . . . Jesus."

I stayed with Donald for a bit, but it felt like I was imposing on his conversation with his Lord. Donald passed that morning at 8:30.

Betty: I Miss My Husband

Betty arrived from a local hospital late in the evening with a diagnosis of a dissecting aortic aneurysm. "My legs just gave out on me. My son found me on the bathroom floor, but my legs just wouldn't work. They found the aneurysm in the emergency room, but the risks of surgery at my age, well, forget it. I'm okay with this life being over. When it's my time, it's my time, and I don't want anyone stopping it."

Betty was a beautiful woman who didn't look anywhere near her stated age of eighty-four. She had shining blue eyes and a smile that very quickly won over the whole staff. She had a full head of thick wavy snow-white hair that was meticulously and neatly groomed. She was a mother of eight and had thirty-two grandchildren. When she arrived, she was having significant abdominal pain but had little sensation from her hips down. The hospice physician immediately put her on morphine sublingual (under the tongue) to be given around the clock. She was kept on her anti-hypertensive medications to keep her blood pressure on the lower side, reducing the pressure on the already ballooning aorta. Very soon after, the morphine had to be increased and given more frequently to control her pain. Within a short amount of time, her pain became minimal, and she was very comfortable. That night, her call bell sounded.

"Come in here, dearie," she said as she waved me into her room.

"Yes, ma'am, what can I do for you?"

"I want to ask you some questions. Do you have time?"

"For you, Betty, I have all the time in the world." I pulled up a chair and sat close to her bed. She straightened up the blanket covering her lap, creasing the top fold with her hands. In her left hand were her favorite silver rosary beads.

"Lately, it hurts to eat. I eat because my children want me to keep eating, but as soon as it hits my intestines and things start rolling around, my pain gets so bad. My question is, I want to know if I can stop . . . stop eating?"

"Have you skipped any meals?"

"Yes, dearie, I skipped breakfast and lunch and felt fine. Dinner came around when my children were here, and they wouldn't let up until I ate something, and so I did. Now I'm paying for it. I had to take extra medicine this evening for pain and nausea, and I was miserable. I don't want to have to go through that all the time, so can I stop?" She looked up at me, her hands neatly clasped together on her abdomen.

"Betty, if eating increases your pain and nausea and causes discomfort, and you want to stop, that's okay. But if you ever want anything to eat, you just let us know, and we can try again with soft, easily digestible food."

"Okay, now what about water? Can I give that up too?"

"Does water cause you pain?"

"No, but I just don't want to drag this out."

"Well, the ability to drink naturally declines on its own. If you want to give up eating because it causes pain, that's different. Your ability to take in fluids as things progress will stop eventually. I think you would be more comfortable taking in water and fluids until you physically can't any longer."

"Okay, that makes sense. Now, tell me something? If I become unconscious, will you still give me pain medicine? How do you take care of me when I can't do anything for myself?"

I explained to her that pain medications would continue to be given, but by a different route. I explained the subcutaneous catheters that would be placed and went into the med cart and brought her one to see what it looked like. I explained that every few hours, we would come into her room and reposition her, and swab out her mouth to keep her oral cavity moist and comfortable. We would put salve on her lips to keep them moist, and we would continue to bathe her and keep her linens and nightgown clean and dry. I explained that the catheter that was in her bladder now would remain there, and that we were able to care for all of her needs even though she wasn't able to.

"And if I . . . you know . . ." Then putting her hand near her mouth, she whispered, "If I have to poop, what then?"

I smiled at her and explained that we could easily clean her up, and change her entire bed even with her in it and her being completely unconscious.

"Some job you have, dearie, wiping the baggy butt of an old woman." She reached over and patted my hand, smiling ear to ear.

"Well, they all look the same, just different sizes and colors, but a butt is a butt," I replied, patting her hand in return.

She laughed. "All right, that sounds fine. But if I don't or can't take water anymore, don't let my children force it in my mouth, okay?" she said, shooting me a quick smile.

"When it comes to that point, we will do our very best to keep you comfortable." Betty looked down at her lap, she caressed the small crucifix of her rosary, then folded her hand around it.

"I'm not scared, you know," she said as she crossed her hands over her belly.

"Not at all?" I asked.

"Not in the least bit. I miss my husband something fierce. I have since the day he died."

"I'm sorry to hear that, Betty. What happened to him?"

"Oh, you don't have time to listen to the stories of this old woman."

I giggled, reached over, squeezed her hand, and said, "Betty, I'd love to hear your stories." I scooted my chair closer to her bed, leaning in intently to listen.

"Well, then, I'll just start at the beginning. My Charlie was the love of my life. I had gone off to college, and in my first semester, that's when I met him—the fall of 1944. Thankfully his feet were as flat as a slab of ham, so he was never a candidate for military duty. Anyway, I was an Education major, and Charlie was studying to be an architect. I was heading to class and he came running around the corner behind me, arms full of books, and plowed right into me. He knocked me flat out on the floor!" She giggled to herself then continued, "He was a good man, but perpetually late, and clumsy as a bag of bricks. We were married after two years of courting and I immediately got pregnant, and that was it. Once the babies started arriving, it didn't stop for quite awhile, but I loved every minute of it." She smiled, opened her hand, and adjusted the beads encircled in the palm of her hand. "I adored being a mom, and Charlie loved being a dad." She folded her hands together, raised her head, and sighed. "He worked at a local company down in the city, but his boss was an unkind man. Charlie did his best to please him, but some people, well, they just aren't happy no matter what. Eventually, he found a job with a firm in southern New Jersey. He left one morning, eager to get up there and find us a home and get settled in. He was going to send for all of us once he found a house, but I never saw him again."

"Oh no, Betty! What happened?" I gasped.

Betty nodded, folded her arms across her tummy, and paused for a moment. "Three weeks after he got up there, he said that he finally found the perfect house that was big enough for all of us and was heading over to sign some papers. That's the last time we spoke. He was hit by a drunk driver just off the curb in front of the home he had just rented for us, and he was killed instantly." She bowed her head, as if recalling that terrible moment. She opened her hands, and caressing the crucifix of her rosary, she sighed, "That was Friday, April 27, 1962, and I'll never forget it."

"Betty, that's awful."

"So there I was, without a husband, seven children and one on the way. You see, I found out I was pregnant the day of Charlie's funeral. Most people thought it was awful, but I saw it as Charlie's last gift to me, another little baby for me to cherish. That's him right there." She picked up a framed photo of her and all her children together. "He's named Charlie, not junior, just Charlie." She caressed the glass over the picture and then set it back in its place on the nightstand.

"I worked all my life, harder than I suppose I had to, but I had to be both a mother and father, you understand. I couldn't do anything less, and I couldn't let Charlie down because I knew he was up there watching over us. Once the life insurance policy ran out, I worked as a secretary for a lawyer three blocks from my home. My oldest children helped watch the young ones, which made it a little easier. My boss was very understanding, especially when the younger children got sick. He proposed to me, you know . . ."

"Your boss did?" I asked.

"Yes, he did, but I said no. Not a day has gone by that I haven't missed my Charlie. Marrying again would have been impossible for me to do. You see, nobody would have been able to fill Charlie's shoes, and I would have felt unfaithful if I had married again. He's waiting for me, I know he is, and . . ." She looked up, small tears welling up in her eyes. "You see, my dear, once you've been married to the finest man, and that's what my Charlie was, nobody else will do."

"That's a beautiful and a sad story, Betty. And, yes, you will see him again."

"I already have." She smiled at me, scanning my expression for disbelief.

"Aw, you did? When?"

"Two nights ago, he walked through that door. He looked just as I remembered him, young and handsome. If I could have, I would have flown up out of this bed. He came over and sat at the foot of my bed." Tears glistened in her eyes as she looked over at me. "I asked him if I could go with him, but he just smiled and said, 'Not yet, Bettums, but very soon.'"

"Betty, how sweet!"

"I've missed him for so long, and it's coming soon, my death, you know. Just a few more days now, I can feel it. But I'm ready, and

I've yearned for it for so long. Now that all of my babies are raised and on their own, it's okay for me. I can move on. So many years of struggling, working my fingers to the bone for them, and I did the best job I could, but I'm tired and I'm ready. They'll be just fine, and so will my grandchildren."

"I'm glad you got to see Charlie again. Do me a favor, will you?" I asked as I reached over and squeezed her hand.

"My dear, you've been so kind to this old woman, anything you want."

"When you get to heaven, and you meet Jesus face-to-face, say a little prayer for me, would you?"

"I will, I absolutely will, my dear." Betty put her arms up, inviting a hug, and I leaned in and gave her a big bear hug.

Betty died suddenly at 2:00 AM the following morning, as her aneurysm no doubt ruptured. She had been having significant pain and then started coughing up blood. She looked up toward the end of her bed as I was hooking up the suction machine, and her eyes opened wide. She smiled, then became unconscious and slipped away before any of her children made it in. By the expression on her face, Charlie no doubt came to retrieve his bride.

Mark: Get Me Out of Here!

"Get me out of here! I have to get away! Help me! Help me!"

I heard those cries as I stepped off the elevator to begin my shift. The day-shift nurse walked out of his room, and while she was giving me report, she said, "Nothing I have given him has helped. We've upped his doses, but nothing is touching his agitation." After the narcotic count was completed, I went first into Mark's room.

Mark was a forty-four-year-old man who came in from home earlier in the week with metastatic renal cell carcinoma. He had a long history of alcohol and drug abuse, and was the youngest of three. He had estranged himself from his two older sisters years ago because of his addictions. His father died of cirrhosis of the liver eight years prior, and his mother died of a stroke two years after his father. His sister Margie was sitting at his bedside, nervously trying to calm him down, when I entered the room to start my shift. Mark was a man who looked many years older than forty-four. His hair was sparse and gray, and his large brown eyes, sunken and hollow, were staring at the left corner of the room and were darting back and forth. He was emaciated with significant temporal wasting, and his abdomen was large, firm, and dreadfully distended. As I put my stethoscope on his back to listen to his lungs, visible tumors resembling grape clusters were easily seen beneath his skin. His hands and feet were puffy and pale and very cool to the touch. His respiratory pattern was rapid and irregular, and his heart rate was high, plucking along at 130 beats per minute.

"Get me out of here, dammit! I gotta get away!" He attempted to fling his legs over the side rail and was trying to scoot his bottom toward the edge of the bed, toward Margie. She got up and put his legs back into the bed, and we grabbed the folded draw sheet underneath his bottom and boosted him back to the top of the bed.

"Isn't there anything that you can give him to calm him down? Nothing has worked all day, and I can't take this much more. Please, can't you give him something?"

I went to his medication sheets and looked at the arsenal of medications usually given for pre-death or terminal agitation. I drew up his medications and went back into his room. When I placed the medicine in his mouth, he immediately spit it out at me, cussing at me to "stop it!" Since the oral medications were no longer an appropriate route given his agitation, I phoned our on-call physician. After receiving orders, I reconstituted a very strong anti-psychotic that he ordered, as well as the other medications used for anxiety, pain, and agitation in subcutaneous form. When I entered the room again, Mark was still staring at something in the corner of the room. He was whimpering, and his shoulders heaved as he attempted again to flee. I inserted subcutaneous lines and quickly gave him his medications. I stayed at the bedside until he calmed down a bit and spoke with Margie about his history, where he was before he came into our unit, and so on. Very discreetly, Margie came around to my side and whispered, "I don't know if you know, but Mark has always had a problem with booze and drugs. He's the baby, I'm the oldest, and we have another sister who wants nothing to do with him. Well, truthfully, he estranged himself from both of us. It was only about six weeks ago that he and I got in contact again. I found out through a mutual friend that he had cancer and that it was bad. I went over to his place to see if I could help. What I saw was awful, just awful. There was rotting food on the counters and in the fridge. There was vomit and stool all over the bathroom that had been there for days and days. The place was filthy, and the smell, well, you get the idea. He couldn't keep anything down."

"Didn't he have a home-care agency lined up to help him?" I asked quietly.

"He wouldn't have it, wouldn't even hear of it. Didn't want anyone invading his privacy. I told him that he could come live with me, maybe save some money, and that I would help take care of him. It took some effort, but he finally agreed. I'm no nurse, but I could see he didn't have very long."

"How long had you two been estranged prior to this?" I asked.

"About seven years. I just couldn't do it anymore, seeing him always strung out or drunk, and he wasn't a nice, happy drunk either. Don't know if you knew, but my father died from cirrhosis, bled to death in his bathroom, and died alone. Me, my mom, and my sister found him, and it looked like a murder scene I tell you—blood everywhere! All over the floor, the toilet, the walls. It was something I will never forget, just absolutely awful. Anyway, Daddy died alone, and I thought I couldn't let Mark die alone too. I'm on disability, so I could at least be there to watch out for him."

"He's lucky to have you," I said as I glanced over at her and smiled.

"Well, once he got to my house and I cleaned all his laundry, I was surprised he didn't ask for booze or drugs. He was confused a lot, and I had to watch out for him while he was smoking. I came home one day from getting groceries and found him asleep in the recliner with a burning cigarette in his hand. He could have burned the whole place down and gone up with it, and that's when I took control of things. I hid his cigarettes and lighter from then on. He could only have them when I was there with him."

Mark settled down and stopped his attempts to break free after repeated doses of medication, but he kept his eyes open, staring at the same spot in the corner of his room. Throughout the evening, he repeatedly required medications for pain, agitation, nausea, and anxiety, and in doses larger than normally given. But given his alcohol and drug history, his tolerance was much higher than a non-addicted person.

Margie decided to leave when Mark had drifted off to sleep. "I can't bear to see him like this. Please call me if he starts, you know, getting closer."

"Can I ask you something before you leave?" I asked as we walked out of his room. "Does Mark have any religious affiliation? We have plenty of chaplains that may be able to help him through this."

"We were raised Lutheran, but I don't think he's stepped inside a church since high school. But if you think a chaplain would help, by all means."

I left a voicemail for one of the chaplains regarding Mark immediately after Margie left, but never received a call-back, and the unit was so busy, I didn't have a chance to call again. Around four in the morning, his bed alarm started going off, alerting us that Mark was attempting to get out of bed. The nursing assistant, Julie, and I darted down to Mark's room to find his legs slightly out of the bed. Too weak to make it any further, we pulled him up in the bed, and when I returned with his medications, he kept repeating, "Leave me alone! Go away! I'm not ready!"

"Not ready for what, Mark?" I asked, hoping I would finally get an answer as I injected more medication into his subcutaneous lines.

"I'm not ready to die! Get me out of here! Get me up, get me up!" he screamed as he attempted to shove me out of the way, weakly swatting at me.

"Mark, you can't run away, you're too weak to get up," Julie said to him as we boosted him back up in the bed.

"I'm not ready! You don't understand!" he said, struggling to sit up again.

"Tell me, help me understand." I sat on the bed next to him, blocking the gap between the side rail and the footboard, his only avenue of escape.

"I'm not ready . . . it's awful!" he said, darting a frightened look over toward the corner of the room and heaving another weak attempt to get up.

"Mark, what is awful? Tell me what you see."

"No, no, no! You don't understand!" Mark broke down and started to cry. Whispering out the words in between sobs, he said, "I've done terrible things . . . too much, too much." He stopped momentarily, let out a sigh, and began again, "Get me out of here! Get him away!" He struggled to get out of bed again.

"Who, Mark? Who do you see?"

"No! No! I can't!" He began sobbing. "Help me . . . help me." As he cried, he put his hand up in front of him, directed toward the corner of the room.

"Who are you telling to go away?"

"Get him away from me! Please, I'm not ready," he said as he stared toward the corner of the room. "Oh my god!" Mark whimpered as his sobbing continued. "It's him! He's here for me! Please help me! Get him away! I'm not ready! I'm not ready! Make him go away, please, please, I don't want to go to hell!"

I turned to Julie and told her to page any chaplain the operator could find. Julie ran out of the room, and I stayed with Mark. As his struggle continued, I stood up and leaned over him. I put his face in my hands and said softly, "Mark, shhh. C'mon, honey, shhh . . . That's it." I stroked his face, gently rubbing his temples with my thumbs. "Jesus is bigger and more powerful than anything you see in that corner."

Mark continued to sob. "Help me, please! He can't forgive me! There's no hope for me . . . there's no hope for me." His face was furrowed and sad.

"Yes, there is, Mark, because you're still alive. Don't listen to that creature in the corner because he has no power in front of God. All it takes is for you to tell God that you're sorry."

"You don't understand," Mark replied as his chin quivered with emotion.

"God's mercy is bigger and more powerful than what's in that corner, and He wants to forgive you, Mark, just ask Him."

"I can't," Mark whimpered.

"Say "Jesus, I am so sorry, from the bottom of my heart, for all of my sins, every single one of them. Jesus, please save me!"

"Jesus . . . please," Mark feebly pleaded as soft sobs flowed over his cyanotic and quivering lips. "Please, Jesus, save me," he whispered as large tears trickled from his eyes and across my fingers, which I gently wiped away. "Save me . . . please," Mark repeated over and over.

I stayed near his bed, held his hand, and silently prayed for him. He continued looking at the same spot on the wall, but his furrowed brow was now relaxed, and his sunken eyes remained half opened. I thought initially that maybe this brought him peace, but as I sat next to him praying, I saw him continue in his feeble attempts to escape. Within the hour, the chaplain arrived, and I left the room to give them privacy. After about twenty minutes, he emerged from Mark's room saying that he had calmed down a bit and had drifted off to sleep. Although medications help with physical symptoms such as anxiety and pain, there really aren't any drugs for spiritual distress. It is my belief the only antidote for that kind of distress is prayer.

Mark died that morning at 10:30.

Bobbie: I Baked Jesus a Pie

The bed alarm sounded, and the nursing assistant and I ran into Bobbie's room. We found her standing butt-naked in front of the window, looking out. She had her hands in front of her, palms up, and appeared to be holding something that we couldn't see.

"Bobbie, dear, are you okay?" I said as I approached her.

"Yes, I am." She smiled. "I'm waiting."

"What are you waiting for, my dear?" I asked as she looked out the window at the darkened horizon lit only by a full moon.

"Well, Jesus, of course. He promised He'd be coming here tonight to get me. I'm just checking to see if He's on His way," she said as she peered out the window, looking in all directions.

"Well, honey, Jesus knows everything, and He'll know exactly where to find you. Let's go back to the bed because you're a little wobbly standing here, okay?" I gently took her by the elbow.

"Be careful! I don't want to drop this pie."

"A pie?" I asked.

"Yes, my dear, I promised Jesus that I would bake him a pie and that I would have it ready for Him when He comes for me. Then we would each have a slice before He takes me home to heaven."

"Here, let me take the pie, and I'll put it on the table over there, and we'll get you back into bed."

"Be careful because it's still very hot," she warned as she stiffened her elbows close to her sides, looking down at her palms. I gently took the invisible pie from her hands and handed it to Julie, who carefully carried the pie and placed it on the over-bed table as Bobbie watched her every move. I helped her back to bed, but she insisted on sitting up for a while. We placed her in the recliner and brought the "pie" near her.

"I need my air! I can't find my air!" I traced the oxygen tubing from the outlet in the cupboard near her bed and found it underneath the pad she was sitting on in the chair.

"Oops, I found it, we're sitting on it. Okay, lean to the left, now to the right. Okay, here it is, Bobbie. I think we were blowing oxygen into the wrong end!" She giggled at me as I placed the prongs into her nostrils. "Now, if this smells like a fart, we'll know why, won't we?" I smiled at her. Bobbie giggled and grabbed me and hugged me close.

"Thank you so much for coming to visit me today. I've been very lonely."

Bobbie was a seventy-six-year-old widow who had two children. She was a very thin woman, with medium-length gray hair that was disheveled and splayed in every direction. She had large deep-brown eyes, and her skin was sallow and pale. Her son, Jeremy, had died eight years ago after losing a battle to ALS. She lived with her daughter, Sara, in an in-law suite built off their home. Bobbie had end-stage lung cancer with metastasis to her liver and bone. She moved in with Sara because she could no longer manage the steps in her home. Bobbie's husband, Ken, had died many years ago from heart failure. They had owned a small bakery for forty-two years, and her husband "baked the most delicious bread and rolls, but *my* specialty was the sweets." She talked about her pie recipes and how she had developed each one from scratch, beginning to end. She said how she loved to see the reactions of the people when they took their first bites.

"If I could get them to come in and try any of my pies, I knew they'd be back—they couldn't help themselves."

Once Bobbie was settled into her chair and her breathing eased, I sat and talked to her for a while to make sure she was going to be okay, while Julie fetched the tab alarm that would alert us should she get up unassisted.

"Tell me about this pie that you made? It smells wonderful."

"Oh, it's my own recipe. It's a hand-made banana cream pie and was always my favorite. Ken adored my pumpkin whipped pie, but I love graham crackers. You know, I always bake from scratch, and I make my own graham crackers that make up the crust. It's delicious, would you like a slice?"

"Oh no, that's the pie that you're saving for Jesus, and it needs to be perfect for Him."

She looked over at me and smiled and said, "You're right, it does. I'm very anxious to see Him." She sighed.

"Tell me, Bobbie, what did He say that led you to believe that He was coming tonight?" I asked as I reached over and squeezed her hand.

"Before I came here, He came to my home. He said He would come back very soon to bring me home to heaven. I asked many times when it would be, but all He would do was smile and say 'Soon.' Then last night, I saw Ken, and he said that Jesus would come for me tonight. I keep looking for Him, but He's nowhere. The pie is ready, and I'm waiting." She looked intently toward the window again, bobbing her head left and right, searching the horizon.

Now, there was nothing in her physical assessment that would indicate that she was anywhere near close to death, especially tonight, but I've heard many patients tell me that they were going to die on a certain day, and many, many times, they were accurate. Initially, I thought she was just confused, but after talking to her and hearing the details, I was concerned enough that I thought I should phone her daughter.

"Mom's been talking crazy lately. We were just there a few hours ago, and she looked fine, so no, I'm not coming back in tonight. Tell her I'll see her in the morning."

At ten o'clock, I went into Bobbie's room to get her back into bed for the night and found her asleep in her chair. I woke her up, and she startled awake and said, "Is it time? Is Jesus here?"

"No, I'm sorry, He's not, but let's get into bed where you'll be more comfortable. When Jesus comes, He'll wake you up, okay?"

Bobbie smiled, and I assisted her into the bed. Although she was weak and wobbly, she managed without too much difficulty. I tucked her in, and she put up her arms to hug me. I leaned over and hugged her. "God bless you, sweet lady," I whispered into her ear.

"God bless you too. I won't be here in the morning, so I'll say good-bye now." She beamed a beautiful smile up at me as she squeezed my hands.

"Good-bye, Bobbie, and when you get to heaven, please pray for me?" I squeezed her hands and kissed them.

"I will . . . I will," she said as I rolled the over-bed table near her.

"Everything's ready. Do you need anything else before I go?"

"Could you get me two glasses of ice water?"

"One for you and one for Jesus?" I asked.

"Oh, yes, yes, thank you." She smiled as she snuggled into her pillow, pulling her blankets up near her chin. I went and filled two large cups with ice water, and Bobbie was asleep when I went back into her room. I placed both cups on her over-bed table, added two forks and two napkins, and then turned out the lights. I continued to check on her frequently during the night, and she was sleeping peacefully, occasionally turning from side to side. At 3:00 AM, I went in again to check on her, but as I neared her doorway, I didn't hear her usual soft snore. I turned on the light, and she was on her back, her hands folded across her lap, the two cups and silverware still sitting on the table, but she was gone. I phoned her daughter, who was completely shocked. When she came in, I told her what Bobbie had requested before she went to sleep and pointed to the two glasses of water and the utensils still sitting on her over-bed table.

"I thought she was talking out of her head. I thought it was the cancer that made her see and say these things . . . did you think she would die tonight?" she asked as she approached the bed.

"Truthfully, no, I didn't. But many times, patients have told me the day they would depart this world, and the majority were right on. I've learned to listen to them because sometimes I think they really know."

"Wow. Well, at least she's with Dad and Jeremy. She was ready, and she'd been telling me for weeks that she was done and tired of living without Pop. Well, Mom," she said as she leaned over her mother and tearfully kissed her forehead, "say hello to Dad and Jeremy for me."

After we phoned the funeral home, Sara stayed until they arrived. As they brought the stretcher into the room, Sara turned to me and said, "I don't want to watch this. Thank you and all the other nurses for the wonderful care you all gave my mom, I really appreciate it." She hugged me and left the unit. As I cleared the room and stripped the bed, I found a small prayer card with a picture of Jesus holding a lamb over his shoulders. Jesus kept His promise to Bobbie and came for her that night, just like she said He would.

Margaret: Don't Let Me Die Alone

Margaret was a fifty-one-year-old woman who had metastatic uterine cancer. She put off surgery and believed solely in a natural approach to her health. She went to herbalists, acupuncturists, and explored many other holistic avenues. She ended up going back to her oncologist when she began having heavy vaginal bleeding accompanied by significant lower back pain. She was immediately sent to the emergency room and was found to be very anemic, requiring blood transfusions to stabilize her very low blood pressure. From there she was rushed to surgery for a total hysterectomy. The surgical report was grim, as hers was an aggressive cancer that had spread outside the uterus, mangling the fallopian tubes and invading the intestines. Large sections of her small and large intestine were removed, and she was given a colostomy. The surgeons attempted to de-bulk the tumors and save as much viable tissue as possible, but in the end, they closed her up and sent her to recovery. Her scans showed the cancer had invaded the liver and lung and was eating its way into her pelvic bones. Palliative radiation was done with little effect. Margaret was unable to return home and was advised to "get her affairs in order" as hospice was her only alternative. She was given less than a week to live.

The night she arrived on our unit, she was in so much pain it was heartbreaking to witness. As her stretcher rolled down the hallway, her white knuckles were visible as her hands clenched tightly to the side rails. Her brow was furrowed, and her eyes were wrought with fear as her chin quivered in pain. Her dark and very curly hair was short and was saturated with sweat. She was deathly pale and diaphoretic from head to toe, which saturated her gown and bed linens. From her abdomen to her feet, she was grossly edematous, and the skin on her legs was tight and shiny. Any pressure applied in these areas left deep indents as massive amounts of fluid pooled and saturated the interstitial spaces. When transferred into the bed, she moaned loudly in terrible pain. Immediately I phoned the doctor, and medications were ordered. After many adjustments and obtaining little relief, her pain medication was transferred to a PCA (patient controlled analgesia) pump that was connected to a needle inserted into her port. This would allow her to push a button to give herself extra medication should she need it. Soon her pain was well managed, and she was finally able rest.

Margaret was a soft-spoken woman who never asked for anything. She rarely put on her call bell and very often preferred to be alone. The cancer had eaten away through the vaginal wall, causing a fistula to develop between the tumor in her abdominal cavity and her vagina. (A fistula is an abnormal connection between two organs or areas that normally don't connect.) This was accompanied by a very malodorous vaginal discharge. Despite everything that was attempted to help, nothing seemed to make a dent in the smell. An electronic room deodorizer was placed in her room to help with the odor, but even with it set to the highest setting, the underlying odor was always present. Because of this, her friends found it very difficult to visit her. Torn between their love for their friend and their inability to stomach the smell for very long, they stayed for only short periods and often were found in tears outside of her room. Finally, Margaret told them, "Please don't come back until it's over. I don't want your last memories of me to be this. Go home, pray for me, and don't worry. I love you, but I don't want you here."

After much discussion between them and many, many tears, they left clinging to each other and sobbing down the hallway and onto the elevator. Two days later, I came back on duty and met the nursing assistant, Julie, near the basement elevators. She smiled, said her usual, "Hey, girl!" and we walked onto the elevator.

"How's Margaret in room 8 doing?"

"Not good. She's been having a lot of pain."

After report, we began our rounds. When we walked near Margaret's room, we heard her crying. We went into her room and initially were overcome with the smell, but we saw her sobbing in bed, sobbing so hard she couldn't speak. I was overwhelmed watching her and couldn't hold back the tears myself. I immediately reached under her shoulders and pulled her toward me. I wrapped my other arm around her and put my head on hers and hugged her. Softly stroking her hair, I said, "It's okay, Margaret. It's okay, honey. What's wrong?"

"Nobody will come in my room anymore. I know I smell . . . Do they think that I can't smell myself? But I don't want to die alone. Please don't let me die alone." She struggled with each syllable, moaning and grunting out her words. I was heartbroken to hear her desperation and her pain. I held her and promised her she would not die alone and promised her we'd be with her every step of the way. As difficult as it was, I held on to her as the smell was akin to that of rotting gangrene. It's a smell that sticks and stays in your nostrils long after you leave the room.

"Margaret, are you in pain?" I asked as I let go of her, still holding on to her hands.

"I'm in terrible pain. Can you get me something?" I gave her a bolus on her PCA pump and increased her basal rate. I left her with Julie and went to fetch her medications. When I returned, I brought her something for anxiety, which she agreed to take. When the meds kicked in, we changed the dressings underneath her and the pads covering the bed. We cleaned her well and packed layers of absorbent pads underneath her. I sprinkled a powdered medication onto her perineal area, which significantly reduced the smell, at least for a time. After fifteen minutes or so, she drifted off to sleep. Around

2:30 AM, it was obvious that the tumors had invaded an artery in her bowel, and she began bleeding rectally, and bleeding huge amounts.

"It's getting closer, isn't it? I'm going to die soon, aren't I?" she whispered.

"Yes, yes, you are. Is there anything else I can do for you?" I asked as I caressed the side of her cheek.

"Pray . . . Pray with me," she whispered back. Together we all said the Lord's Prayer, and then Julie led us in a spontaneous, beautiful, and touching prayer. Margaret smiled and looked over at Julie with an expression of gratitude that melted our hearts. Julie leaned over and hugged her, kissed her cheek, and said, "God loves you more than you could ever imagine. He will take very good care of you."

Margaret nodded and then closed her eyes. Within minutes, she expelled a huge amount of blood that, before we could get to it, began dripping off the edge of the bed. Margaret moaned softly as we quickly covered the blood with blankets and towels to quickly sop it up. Julie and I never left her side, and we held her hands until her final breath a few minutes later. Margaret did not die alone, and we were with her every step of the way, as promised.

Father Pete: Waiting at the Door

"I loved being a priest. It was the best job in the world," he said in his thick Irish brogue. Father Pete was eighteen when he entered the seminary, straight out of high school. A large smile grew over his face as he recalled his vocation and his many years in service to his parish and community. "When the bone cancer hit, well, it was no big deal . . . Really, just no big deal. I'm an old man, and I'm ready to die. I've been preparing for it me whole life, and I welcome brother death with open arms."

Father Pete came to our unit when he could no longer stay in his parish rectory. Although he was only sixty-nine, he insisted that he be allowed to continue with his duties until he physically couldn't handle them any longer. When it came to the point that he could no longer walk without excruciating pain, he spoke to his oncologist about it. PET scans found his pelvis bones were riddled with cancer, deteriorating the bone because of the invading cancer. Now wheelchair- and bed-bound, he opted to enter our facility in order not to burden his fellow priests, with whom he lived.

"I knew from the time I was in the fourth grade that I was going to be a priest. It's all I've ever wanted to do, and for the past fifty-one years, I have done the best job I could in serving my Lord. But lately, for about the last six months or so, I've had to reign in me duties because getting around was just too difficult. I put in the bulletin that I would have to refrain from saying Mass, performing marriages and baptisms. Even hearing confessions was difficult because of the back and hip pain. And now, I've been in here for ten days, and do you know that I received a call from a young woman saying, 'Please, Father Pete, can you baptize me baby?' I can't even wipe me own arse much less baptize a wee baby." We couldn't help but laugh out loud. Father Pete was a remarkable man, and he always insisted that we come into his room before we went home to receive his blessing. He always had a smile, a gentle touch on your hand, and an ear always ready to listen to anything you had to say. When you were in the room with Father Pete, nobody else mattered. You were the only person he focused on, and he never forgot a face or a name even after only one meeting.

Time passed, and Father Pete grew weaker and weaker. One night at the beginning of my shift, Julie and I went into his room. He was sitting up in bed and smiled when he saw us.

"Come here, girls, come here," he said softly as he waved his hand at us, bidding us to come closer. 'Tonight, I want you to give me *your* blessing." Such a request left both of us surprised.

"Father Pete, are you sure?" I asked.

"Absolutely! Doesn't need to be anything fancy, but please . . ."

"Okay. Father Pete, may God bless you tonight, tomorrow, and always."

"That'll do! I'll take that!" Father Pete said as he took my hand. Julie, who was on duty with me that night, was much more comfortable praying out loud in front of others. Julie went on and said the most beautiful blessing, and Father Pete smiled from ear to ear.

"Thank you both, that was wonderful!"

We repositioned Father Pete back in his bed. He thanked us again, and we continued our rounds. Around 2:00 AM, Father Pete put on his light. When Julie and I entered his room, he whispered, "Do you think you could get me up to the recliner? I think I'll feel better sitting in the chair."

"Absolutely, Father, anything you want."

We pulled up the recliner close to the bed, locked the wheels, and lowered his side rails. He was so weak and could hardly bear any weight, but he helped as best he could. We lifted him up and very gently put him in the chair. Once we settled him in, he said, "I'm so tired . . ."

"It's very difficult, Father, this last part of the journey," I said as I took his hand, giving it a squeeze.

"You have no idea . . . I am beyond exhausted. Do you think that you could wheel me chair over there so that I'm facing the door?"

We cleared a path, moving away the bedside tables and other chairs, and pushed his chair over to the end of the bed. We angled it up against the wall so that he was facing the door. I put his night-stand and call bell near him. I heard a call light alarm in the hallway, and Julie darted out of the room to answer it.

"Anything else I can do for you, Father?"

"Could you comb me hair and wipe me face, please?"

I wet his hair and combed it smooth. I also took a warm wash-cloth and wiped his face. I offered him a sip of water, which he refused. I walked over to the cupboard and put his comb back in his basin. When I walked back over to him, he was staring at the door-way. His eyes were wide open, fixed on the doorway, and he started to smile. "Father, are you okay?" I asked as I touched his shoulder. He continued to look at the doorway for about ten seconds or so, his expression unchanging, bright and joyful. Then his head dropped back onto the recliner, his face looked up at the ceiling, and he closed his eyes halfway. A few slow, deep breaths followed, and he died.

I believe Father Pete knew that he would soon meet his Lord. In retrospect, having his face washed and his hair combed, ready to meet the God whom he had served all of his life, only seemed appro-priate. I will never forget the expression on his face, one of anticipa-tion, surprise, and great joy.

Jack: The Colors Are Incredible

J ack was a seventy-eight-year-old male with metastatic prostate cancer. He was admitted into our unit initially as a respite patient. Respite patients come in once a month and stay for five days in order to give the families caring for them a much-needed rest. Jack was tall, over six feet, thin, and very pale. After a two-day stay with us, he was having more and more difficulty urinating, his pelvic pain was increasing, and he became weaker. He was changed from a respite patient to inpatient status, and a catheter was inserted into his bladder to relieve his discomfort. Large amounts of urine returned, and his discomfort was immediately relieved. After my initial assessment, he asked for the bedside commode to move his bowels. He said he was up earlier in the day and did just fine. We struggled to get him up, and he was surprised that he could no longer bear much weight. When we returned him to his bed, I told him, "Jack, honey, your legs are very weak, and it is unsafe for us to continue getting you up to the commode. I sure as heck don't want to drop you."

"I know, I'm sorry. I was able to stand this morning. My legs just can't do it anymore, I guess. It's okay, I will take the bedpan from now on." He looked down at his lap and sighed, as if disappointed in himself.

"We could use the lift to get you up, which will be safer for you, if you'd like."

"Don't bother with the lift, I'll be fine with the bedpan." He smiled, still looking at his lap. Then he lifted his head, looked at me, and said, "Did you know my wife died here four years ago? Heart failure."

"Oh, Jack, I'm so sorry to hear that."

"I saw her last night." After a pause, he added, "Am I going crazy, or is it my medicine?" He looked up with worry across his face.

"No, you're not going crazy. It is very common for loved ones to show up to help us along the way." I touched his arm reassuringly. "Did she speak to you?"

"Yes, she did. She said she would be back very soon when I'm ready to go. I told her that I'm ready now, but she just smiled. She said, 'Soon, JJ, very soon.' JJ was her nickname for me." He looked up, searching my expression for disbelief.

"How sweet! What did she look like, if I might be so bold as to ask?"

"She looked like she did when she was young and was as solid as you are. I couldn't see through her, if that's what you are asking, but as beautiful as I had always remembered her."

"Was she alone, or did she bring others with her?"

"No, she was alone. I want to go with her. I'm so tired, and I miss her."

"Well, Jack, many times when people we love who have passed start showing up, it's a good sign that it won't be much longer."

"How much longer?" he asked with anticipation in his eyes.

"That's difficult to say. Sometimes it's weeks, days, or just hours."

"I hope it's soon . . . I hope it's soon."

"Are you ready for it, Jack?"

"You mean ready to die? Oh, I've been ready for a very long time. I really don't know what has taken God so long, but now that I know He's on His way, I am very anxious for it, anxious in a good way." He looked up and smiled at me, his fatigue evident in his deep, brown eyes.

When I entered his room the following evening to begin my shift, Jack was sitting up in the bed looking at the crown molding, smiling and watching something I could not see. I looked in the direction he was staring, touched his arm, and said, "Hello." Jack looked over at me and smiled, then immediately went back to watching whatever it was that he saw.

"It's beautiful over there, isn't it?" I asked him.

"The colors! Oh, the colors are incredible!"

He smiled as if captivated by what he saw. He continued watching for hours, and finally, around ten o'clock, he fell asleep. Early in the morning, when I took in his medication and to reposition him again in the bed, he reached over the bed rail and grabbed my elbow. I slipped my hand into his and put my other hand on the side of his face, gently smoothing the hair on his temple.

"Thank you for everything."

"Jack, it was my privilege to take care of you, truly. Thank you for always being so easy to take care of."

"When are you coming back?"

"I'm off until Tuesday."

"Tuesday . . . I won't be here on Tuesday," he smiled.

"You're ducking out before I get back then?" I smiled back, but my heart ached thinking I wouldn't see him again. Jack smiled, and his eyes sparkled. I leaned over and gave him a hug and left for the day.

Jack died that night at 11:40 PM.

Dottie: My Family Is on the Dock

Dottie was a seventy-five-year-old woman who was admitted into our hospice on a stormy Tuesday evening. She arrived accompanied by her daughter, son-in-law, and the ambulance crew. Dottie was a tall heavyset woman with dark hair underlying the silver gray. She had pale blue-green eyes that were weary, sunken, and surrounded by dark circles. We transferred her into the bed, and Julie began changing her out of her hospital gown and into one of our hospice nightgowns. I escorted her family out of the room and gave them a tour of our facility. I had them sign the consent forms and spoke to them about our unit, our routines, and what they could expect as far as care for their mother. They were both very anxious and exhausted, and when Julie had finished Dottie's bath and initial pampering, I took them back into the room to say good-bye for the night.

Dottie had been diagnosed with breast cancer three years earlier and had undergone a bilateral mastectomy. At the beginning of this year, her cancer returned with a vengeance, and after extensive radiation, it was found that her cancer was unrelenting in its progression. Opting for no further treatments, she was enrolled in hospice at the hospital. As I began my assessment of her, I removed the pad that Julie had placed over her wounds to keep her gown clean. Her chest was hyper-pigmented, a brownish-purple color, and she had large, fungating tumors that had erupted through her skin and were oozing serous, bloody fluid. Astonishingly though, Dottie said she had no pain. I cleaned and dressed her wounds, and we tucked her in for the night.

As the days passed, Dottie quickly became a favorite patient, not only to the doctors and nurses, but the ancillary staff and volunteers as well. Always quick-witted, her dry sense of humor endeared her to everyone. Impressively patient as her strength slowly dwindled, she was thoughtful and very appreciative of any care afforded her.

One night, during her bath, she kept looking up at the ceiling. "Do you see anyone, Dottie?" Melody, the nursing assistant, asked, since Dottie was obviously watching something.

"Yes, I do, I see my family. They're all standing there on the dock," she whispered as she lifted her arm up and shakily pointed toward the ceiling. "I wish I could get to them."

"Is Jesus there too?" I queried. She looked up at the ceiling for a bit then sighed.

"No." She shook her head slowly, and her face melted into a sadness of expression that touched my heart.

"Don't worry, Dottie, when you see Jesus standing on the dock, then it'll be your time to go. Is anyone else there?"

"A bunch of people, but I don't know them. We're all standing in a line."

"Are many people in front of you?"

"One, two, three . . . there's eight people in front of me."

"Don't worry, Dottie, it'll be your turn when you get to the front of the line."

Days passed, and Dottie remained the same, intermittently staring up at the ceiling watching the progression of the line. One particular evening was extremely busy; we had admitted a very unstable man into the unit who was actively dying upon arrival, and two hours later, he passed. Afterward, when I went to check on Dottie to change her position, we found her crying.

"Dottie, what's the matter honey? Why are you crying?" I asked, leaning over her, caressing her shoulder.

"A man just came and took my place in line. I was getting so close, and he was put in front of me." I'm not sure how she could have known, or if it was our patient who took her place in line, but to say the least, we were shocked by her answer.

"Dottie, do you still see your family?"

"Yes, they're still there, and they're smiling at me."

"They'll wait for you, dear, they won't go until you get to the front of the line, then you can go with them." Dottie looked over at me and smiled.

"Jesus is coming soon. I know He is . . . He's coming," she whispered.

The following night, when I began my rounds, I entered Dottie's room and found her lying on her side, staring at the ceiling with a beautiful smile on her face, and she was moving her lips as though she were speaking to someone. When I went in to begin my physical assessment of her, she lowered her raised arm to her side. I asked her if she was talking to her family. Dottie looked over at me and smiled and gently shook her head no. She looked back up at the ceiling, smiled softly, and whispered, "It's Jesus." She lifted her arm again toward the ceiling, and it stayed suspended in the air for quite some time until fatigue dropped it down by her side again.

"So you're at the front of the line, Dottie?" I asked. She turned her head slowly and looked at me and nodded. I finished her assessment and phoned her family and told them what Dottie had said.

Dottie passed that night, at 11:04 PM, with a smile on her face and her family at her side.

Karyn: Get Out of My Way

Stage IV thyroid cancer is something that isn't easy to hear for anyone, but it was particularly difficult for Karyn. A mother of two and only sixty years old, she had devoted her life as a wife, a mother, and a nurse. Battling mental issues for most of her adult life, it was discovered that her thyroid issues had long been ignored by her until the lump in her neck affected her swallowing. She underwent a complete thyroidectomy and received chemo and radiation post-op. Admitted this snowy evening, she had gone to the ER earlier for difficulty breathing. It was discovered that she had quite advanced metastatic cancer.

"Denial is a powerful thing. If I don't think about it, if I can ignore it long enough, it'll go away. It'll go away or kill me, and obviously, it's the latter, isn't it?" she whispered in between periodic pauses to catch her breath. "But I've lived a good life and tried to do some good for other people and my patients, so hopefully that counts for something."

During my first physical assessment of Karyn, it was very obvious that she had put off medical care for a very long time. Large hard masses surrounded the base of her neck near the scar from her previous thyroidectomy. Another large mass was near her collarbone, extending down to the right armpit; this impeded lymph flow, making her right arm double in size from lymph edema. Another tumor protruded from her chest on the lower portion of her sternum, which had broken open and was oozing clear fluid and bloody discharge. According to her reports, her right lung was nothing but tumors and her left had large amounts of fluid accumulated, which the ER had tapped, or drained. Finding there was no further treatment available at this late stage, Karyn told her doctors, "Just let me go, it's my own fault."

Karyn was a strikingly beautiful woman of Irish heritage, with deep, green eyes and dark-auburn hair. Her ever-devoted husband sat silently in a chair near her bed, head lowered, his eyes red from crying. "Don't worry, Billy, it's just my time. It'll be all right."

Bill looked up, glanced over at me, turned to Karyn, and said softly, "I tried everything I could to get her to go back to the oncologist and get checked out, and she has refused for the last four-and-a-half years. That's how long this has been going on, four-and-a-half years!" He reached over and grabbed his wife's hand, and said, "We could have had more time together. I just wanted more time" Tears welled up in his eyes.

"Billy, more time? It would have been awful like it was when I went through chemo the first time. Not having the energy to get out of bed, barfing my guts up, veins that feel like they're full of hot lead searing through my body. No, thank you! I barely got through it the first time, and I knew I couldn't do it again." Squeezing his hand, she whispered, "It'll be all right, honey, you'll be just fine."

After my assessment, we settled her into her room. I accessed her port and provided her with a little morphine to ease her breathing. After Karyn had drifted off to sleep, Bill approached the nurses' station, put his elbows on the counter, folded his gloves in half, and laid them on the countertop in front of him. I looked up and smiled when he said, "I'm going to go home and get some sleep. Please take good care of her, she means the world to me."

"We will," I replied, smiling back at him. Bill then stood up straight, put his gloves on, turned, and walked toward the door. He paused before he opened the door. He looked down toward the floor, took a deep breath, and then pushed open the door and walked out with heavy shuffling steps.

For the next several days, Karyn steadily declined, requiring more and more medications to control her symptoms and her pain. She slept for longer and longer periods, and slowly began refusing food, save for a bite here and there and a couple of sips now and again. One particular evening, she became restless and was attempting to crawl out of bed, setting off the bed alarm. After many tries to keep her in bed, I sat next to her to try and keep her calm. Despite medications for agitation and restlessness, nothing was easing her anxiety.

"Get those people out of my way!" she said, waving her arm, weakly pushing an invisible person in front of her.

"What's going on, Karyn, who's in your way?"

"There's so many people in front of me, and they won't move," she said, her eyelids closed and her head leaning back on her pillow, obviously witnessing something. "There's a whole bunch of them, and no matter how hard I try, they won't let me by. My daddy is over there on the other side of the river, and I need to get to him!" She squealed as she pointed toward the wall front of her. "Can't you get me over there? Can't you make them move?" she said as she attempted again to get out of bed.

"How many people are in front of you?

Karyn stopped and lowered her arms, and keeping her eyes closed and her head lifted toward the ceiling, she began counting. "One, two, three, four . . . there's sixteen! Sixteen people who are all ignoring me!" she whined. "Don't they know I have to get over to Daddy? Don't they see that I need to go?" Karyn lowered herself back onto her pillow and sighed. "I gotta get to my . . . Daddy, I'm coming, I'm trying," she whimpered.

"We have to wait our turn in line, Karyn. Your dad will wait. He'll wait for you, honey, just a little longer," I said as I stroked her long auburn hair. She slowly let go of the side rails and relaxed back onto the bed.

Throughout the night, Karyn could be heard calling out for her dad, but was so weak and easily winded that her attempts to get out of bed lessened. As the days passed, Karyn became more and more lethargic, and grew weaker and weaker. Unable to swallow without difficulty, she pushed the straw away from my hand, saying, "No, no more. Get that away from me . . . makes me sick." Gradually, she became too weak to reposition herself in the bed, so every few hours, we would go in and turn her. She lost the ability to swallow due to the growing tumors, including her own saliva. Frequent mouth care and the addition of sublingual Atropine eased this significantly, but we kept Chux near her mouth to collect the drool that would occasionally ooze from her lips.

Around 2:00 AM, while we were repositioning her, she opened her eyes and looked my direction.

"What is it, honey, are you okay?" Thinking she was going to ask me something, I asked her again. Her eyes did not track mine, and she looked past me. Karyn stared, fixated on something next to me. She slowly smiled, her mouth moved as if speaking to someone, and for quite some time, she continued gazing at someone near her bed. At 3:15 AM, I went in to check on her again, and she had fallen asleep. At 3:42, the lights at the nurses' station flickered. I looked over at Melody, and we both got up and walked into Karyn's room. When we turned on the lights, it was obvious that Karyn had taken the hand of her dad and crossed over to the other side of the river. Her lifeless body remained in the same position we had left her earlier. Her eyes were half open, lifeless and glazed over. We repositioned her onto her back, folded her arms across her tummy, and closed her eyelids. I phoned her husband, who said he couldn't bring himself to see her and asked that we call the funeral home for him. Karyn had finally made it to the front of the line and across the river.

Alan: A Trip to Hell

Alan was a seventy-seven-year-old man who was admitted into our hospice with end-stage bladder cancer that had metastasized everywhere. Despite surgery, chemo, and radiation, the cancer spread unabated. He required a catheter to be placed as soon as he arrived, as he had been unable to urinate for quite some time. I quickly placed his Foley, and it returned large amounts of blood and urine. Knowing frequent irrigation would be needed to keep it from clotting off, I returned to set up all the necessary supplies in the room. When I walked in, his wife Regina, was sitting in a chair next to Alan's bed. They were speaking quietly to each other when he reached up and caressed her cheek. She leaned over and cupped her hands around his, pressing his palm closely onto her cheek. The exchange of affection between them as they looked at each other was so beautiful.

"What are the visiting hours?" Regina asked.

"There aren't any, you can come any time, stay as long as you like, even spend the night if you wish. The couch folds out into a bed." Regina smiled over at Alan, but you could tell she was exhausted, so I left them alone to visit.

Later on, when I went into his room to give Alan his nighttime medications, his wife stood up and announced to Alan that she had to get home but, in the same breath, voiced her desire to stay.

"Regina, dear, I'll be just fine. You're exhausted . . . go home and get some sleep, and I'll see you tomorrow."

Regina leaned over his bed, smothered him with hugs and kisses, and then walked out of the room laden with worry. I gave her our phone number and walked her to the door when she reached over and grabbed my arm, "I'm not ready for this, I'm really not. I wish we had more time." She looked over at me, her eyes reddened with emotion, then turned and walked out the door.

I finished up my duties with all my other patients and then returned to Alan's room. He was a strikingly handsome man with a beautiful head of wavy snow-white hair. He had large hazel eyes surrounded by deep, dark circles, so typical of severe illness. Thick, bushy eyebrows that jutted out in all directions, just screaming for a trim, topped them. He was rather thin, with hands that were thick with calluses from hard and strenuous work.

"I love to garden," he said as he caught me looking at his hands. "There is nothing better than being outside digging in the dirt."

"What did you do before you retired?" I asked.

"Who said I'm retired?" He shot me a quick smile.

"Uh, I just . . ." I stammered.

"I'm just teasing. I was a mechanical engineer. I owned my own company that I built up from nothing. Started out with four employees, and when it sold, we had over two hundred. Its sale afforded me enough money to do all of the things I've wanted to do for so long. Digging in the dirt is one of those pastimes that I thoroughly enjoy. It's how I relax, and I pray a lot when I'm on my knees, pulling weeds." Alan held up his hands in front of him, "These used to be pale and soft, but now look at them, always stained black. I've been tending to the seedlings in my greenhouse, my heaven on earth." He folded his hands across his lap. "So what am I in for tonight from you?"

"Nothing awful, I can assure you. Are you having any pain?"

"No more pain than usual. Pain isn't a bad thing, you understand. It reminds me that I'm still alive." He sighed and pulled his arms up, linking his fingers together, resting them behind his head with his elbows stretched out to the sides.

"Are you uncomfortable now?"

"No, not at the moment. If I get uncomfortable, you'll be the first one I call." Alan leaned back and settled himself onto his pillow.

"Well, if it does get to a point that you're uncomfortable, we have an arsenal of medications to help. Just don't let the pain get too bad before you ask for meds. Pain is much easier to control when it's low, rather than when it's peaked."

"I only have pain when I can't pee, and as you can see, you helped that out quite nicely with this godforsaken thing!" Smiling, he pointed to his catheter tubing. "Dying isn't something to take lightly. I should know—I've been there and done that, as they say."

"Been there? You mean you've died before?"

"Oh, yes, ma'am, I have. Didn't you see my zipper?" He opened his pajama top and pointed to the all-too-familiar white scar down the center of his sternum.

"Yes, I did see that. Is that when you died?" I asked.

"It's a long story, and undoubtedly, you have more pressing matters to attend to. Maybe when you have the time?"

"I have plenty of time and would love to hear your story, if you're up to telling me." I turned to the side and slid a chair next to the bed and sat down.

"Well, it's a long one, I must warn you."

"I don't mind. Please I'd love to hear all of it, if you're up to telling me." I settled back into my chair and crossed my legs.

"Well, should I start from the beginning?"

"Absolutely!" I smiled.

"OK . . . Well, I grew up an only child on a small farm in western Ohio. I was raised Catholic and went to parochial school through the seventh grade, then public school eighth through twelfth. My parents were both very devout, but I grew away from my faith when I lost my best friend in a terrible car accident. I had just turned sixteen, and that incident propelled me into a terrible and angry depression, which progressed to a complete hatred of God. I had no time for Him, no time for any of it. I matured into a rotten man who didn't give a damn about anything or anyone. Selfish to the core, I was completely self-absorbed. Even after I married and had children, I sought my own comfort, my own wealth, me, me, me. I'm telling you the truth now, if it didn't benefit me or increase my bank account, I couldn't give it a second thought. About twenty years ago—twenty-two years and four months ago, to be exact—I needed open-heart surgery. Too many years of rough living, drinking, cigarettes—well, you know the story. The morning of surgery, I was getting ready to go to the hospital. Regina came into the bathroom to comfort and encourage me, as any normal wife would do. I snapped at her, 'Go back to bed, and I'll call you when I need a ride home.'" Alan paused and shook his head. "Nice guy, wasn't I?" He reached over and took a sip of water from the cup on his bedside stand. "So I drove alone to the hospital. After the preliminaries, I was taken on a gurney into the surgical suite. When my anesthesiologist arrived, he introduced himself and sat on a stool at my head, and asked me to repeat my name, date of birth, etc., and I watched him rolling back and forth as he set up his machines. Then he rolled over, looked down at me, and although his face was masked, I immediately noticed his very kind eyes.

"'Okay, Alan, we're about ready to start. Would you like me to pray with you before I put you under?' I looked up at him as anger stirred in my belly, and I laughed out loud, 'You don't believe any of that bullshit, do you? Well, I don't! Just hurry up and put me out and get this over with.' I could feel the medication run hot in my vein, and he asked me to count backwards . . . 100, 99, 98, and then everything went black and completely silent." Alan paused as he looked up at the ceiling. "I woke up and was looking down at my surgeons and wondered, how on earth did I get up here? With that last thought, I was sucked through the ceiling, like a handkerchief being pulled out of a small pocket, and was hurled through a very dark tunnel. At the end of this blackness, I saw what looked like a pinpoint of light, which grew bigger and bigger until it completely surrounded me, and in the center of this light was Jesus." Alan paused, shook his head slightly. "I may have been a self-proclaimed and loud-mouthed atheist, but I knew who Jesus was. So there I was, standing before Him whom I had ridiculed and lashed out at all of my life. There He was—so magnificent and so beautiful." Alan stopped for a moment as tears welled up in his eyes. His voice broke, and he struggled to get the words out. "I was so humiliated. Then pictures of my life began to appear, and I remembered all the insults I used to spew out at every God-fearing person I'd ever encountered. They reverberated in my ears, one after the other after the other. The expression on Jesus's face was one of extreme disappointment and, unbelievably, love. I thought, after all of this, how could He still love me? I stood there before that beautiful but scrutinizing gaze, and I was crushed, crushed by my own sinfulness. I saw my soul as God sees it, you see, and it was appalling. I was covered with holes and a sinful filth that I had willingly accumulated and heaped upon myself, so much that I had become unrecognizable! Like a decaying corpse turned rancid and putrefied, and its weight on my soul pulled me down and screamed out my shame before my God. I should have willingly run as far as I could, but there was nowhere to go. I was stuck solid in place and forced to view it all, without excuse, without relief. I was ashamed of my sinfulness in front of such incomprehensible purity. Oh, dear God, have mercy."

Tears flowed from his eyes as he put his hands up to them, wiping them with the heels of his hands. Pulling a tissue out of the box on his bedside stand, he mopped up the tears and paused for quite some time. With a sharp inhalation, he began again, "Oh, dear God, what have I done? I wanted it to stop so badly. I didn't want Him to see any more of it because, with each and every incident, I felt His disappointment more acutely than I had ever felt anything in my life. I was hoping there was some glimmer of goodness, but with each and every scene, there was nothing. A life wasted—energy expended in the accumulation of tin and brass and nothing of any substance in His eyes. I stood before Him, stripped naked and exposed, like a filthy beggar with nothing to give Him. No merit, no love, no proof of love for Him, only self-love. Empty hands . . . empty soul . . . empty life."

Alan clenched his fist around his tissue, leaned over and tossed it into the trashcan. He reached up and drew another one from the box and wiped his eyes and blew his nose. "Never in my life had I experienced anything like it, and I knew my sentence. I knew without any doubt what my fate was. When my life review had finished, I looked at Jesus. His gaze was one of such inexpressible pity, and His sadness was felt so keenly inside of me that it shattered my soul. Then, as I stood there looking at Him, He closed His eyes and looked down." Alan leaned forward in the bed, looking directly at me. "Now you have to understand something about all of this. When the soul sees Jesus, it is immediately infused with a very powerful and uncontrollable desire to be near Him. He has the most compelling power that pours from Him that you are immediately and completely captivated. But when I saw Him close His eyes and look down, my soul was struck with such an incredible sense of separation that I felt completely shattered. Such overwhelming desperation overcame me, and I threw myself at His feet and started to cry uncontrollably. I apologized with everything that I had in me and begged and begged for another chance. I said, 'Jesus, please! You can do anything! Please give me another chance. I'll change my life, and I'll make it better, I promise! Please, Jesus, don't abandon me!" I lay prostrate at His feet, sobbing for what seemed to be an eternity. Broken-hearted, I lay there surrounded by my own filth, clinging to and kissing the garment that covered His feet. But," Alan said as he shook his finger at me, "I knew more than I knew anything that this judgment was just. I deserved hell and knew it was where I belonged. Jesus lifted me up and looked directly at me, and in His gaze, all of my sins began to quickly melt away and crash into nothingness, like icicles beneath a warm winter sun. All of my hatred and selfishness drained from inside of me, and I was left empty and full of holes, a tattered remnant of a once-pure soul. He put his arms around me and pulled me to His heart, and next to His heart, I felt the warmth of His love so completely and His forgiveness so thoroughly that I was overwhelmed with emotion and began to sob like a baby. He held me for quite some time, and into my soul, He poured His love and forgiveness, consuming my nothingness, sweeping me up into a love that was so intense it enveloped me in an indescribable peace. My tattered and empty soul was instantly made whole. The grime and filth were replaced with a luminous beauty. Oh, I can't describe how incredible a soul appears that is restored to grace and purified. It is the most beautiful thing I have ever seen, and it reflects back to Him a resplendent light. I saw instantly how every soul is precious, and what a wonder and a perfect creation each one is. I was overcome with the immensity of His love for me, and I could have stayed in His embrace forever. Then His words entered my mind and He said, 'I will give you another chance, but first, I want you to see what would have been your eternity this very day.' He called out, and two beings immediately arrived and stood behind me. The one on my right felt very familiar, and I learned intuitively that it was my guardian angel. The being on my left was very large and absolutely beautiful, and radiated majestic strength. This was St. Michael, the big angel, the Archangel." As he said this, Alan lifted his arms up and extended them outward to show me Michael's size. "Both angels were very large and very strong, but Michael was magnificent, beautiful beyond description—just stunning! Jesus placed His hands on my shoulders, He looked into my eyes, and I knew this was good-bye. I was overcome with sadness, as I would have given anything to stay with Him. Then instantly"—Alan snapped his fingers—"we were standing in a barren valley, completely desolate and surrounded by huge black mountains that were jagged and sharp. Their base was deeper than the path we were standing on, extending to depths that seemed to have no end, no bottom. We walked along this very wide path, and at first it was smooth and flat, but as we walked along, it descended and became very steep and very slippery. I was afraid I would fall because on each side of this pathway were horrible-looking creatures crawling up from the darkness. They growled and hissed as their sharp-clawed hands snatched at my heels. I was trying to keep away from them when one looked up at me, then said in a voice that was terrible and penetrating, 'Alan . . . we've been waiting for you!' The fear that rushed through me was like nothing I have ever experienced, and I wanted to run, but my angels urged me on. The deeper we went, the heavier the atmosphere became. In the distance, I heard very faintly a terrible ruckus—fighting, arguing, and screaming. As we continued, the noise increased in volume. I didn't want to go any further as panic rose within me, and although supported on either side by my angels, my steps slowed as my reluctance grew. Michael then said to me, 'You must see what awaits sinners who reject God.'

"We continued farther down this path toward an immense and living blackness. At the end of our descent was a huge and formidable-looking structure that seemed to go on forever both in depth and height. Immense gates were closed at the entrance, secured with enormous black bolts from the outside. Michael raised his hand, and the bolts released and the gates opened. Immediately, a sickening stench filled my nose that both burned and nauseated me. Like rotting flesh in the heat of a summer sun, soaked in burning tar and sulfur. It was terrifying, and I was so frightened but was supported by my angel. As the gates opened, the sounds that hit my ears made me tremble with fear. Ear-piercing screams and language that was so utterly filthy, I would never repeat it to anyone. The cacophony of screams, blasphemies, and continual weeping and wailing filled the air and reverberated through me, filling me with an indescribable terror. As we entered this horrible place, I saw cells of varying heights and depths lining the walls, and each cell contained one soul. I was given an instant knowledge of each soul I saw imprisoned here. Intuitively I knew in what era they had lived, a little bit about their life, and the circumstances that led to their condemnation. To my right I saw a dreadful black wall that extended to dizzying heights. Within this wall, which appeared to be made out of a coal-like stone, small niches were carved. One niche on top of the other, thousands upon thousands of them, and they extended the length and height of this wall. Each one was of similar size, circular in shape, and each contained a soul that was crammed into it. These souls were unable to move, unable to adjust themselves for any comfort. Their faces were flattened and turned outward toward the center of this dungeon, and they wailed, screamed, and cursed continually. Wide bulging eyes with expressions of tortured despair so excruciating that I had to look away.

"'Look!' my angel said. 'Look!' The regret that filled each and every one of them was without respite and ate at them continually. I could see the cause of their torture, as their lives continually played out before them, stopping at specific times showing a particular episode, a particular sin. They screamed out insults at God, cursing names of parents, lovers, even their own children. Scenes over and over, not only of their own sins but the affect those sins had on other people. I was shown the hurt they caused, how their words and actions cut down and destroyed other people. If another soul ended up in this abyss because of their actions or poor example, they were held responsible for that soul to an extent, which intensified their sufferings twofold, threefold, or however many souls were damned because of them. Demons in the most hideous forms, some half-animal, some looking somewhat human, stood near the faces of certain souls who were screaming out at them from their compartment. These demons grabbed the faces of certain tortured souls and pried open their mouths with their claws, so wide that it ripped the flesh along the sides of their cheeks. Then they vomited into their mouths, shoving their mouths closed as the fiery vomit burned them from the inside out. Those poor souls became white, like molten metal, as the demons slammed them deeper into their slim-fitting pit of torture, hurling hideous insults at them.

"At the very bottom of this immense wall lay one niche that was empty. Standing in front of it was a huge and horrible demon, and I felt its gaze sear into me as I turned in its direction. It pointed to me, then to the empty hole, and I knew immediately that this pit was reserved for me. I was overwhelmed with terror and began screaming as I attempted to flee, clawing at my angels who held me steadfast, attempting with all of my strength to run away. This display of sheer terror on my part only incensed its hatred as it lunged at me, threw its arms toward me, but its claws missed me by a fraction of an inch. My angel held me close and calmly reassured me that God's mercy had not only prevented me from staying here, but would also guard against any attack by any of the creatures in this place. I felt an immediate relief as his words entered my mind, but I still couldn't take my eyes off of that creature as he continued to watch me. 'Safe now, but not always,' it grumbled, as deep, hate-filled eyes remained fixed on me. The angels steered me away, but I could still hear its guttural growls as we continued on our way. As we descended farther into this abyss, I saw a desolate-looking wall lined with cells. In one particular cell was a horrific soul, covered with disease and completely filthy. As we got closer to this cell, I learned that this particular man while on earth manipulated, abused, and forced women into prostitution. I saw that he was a cruel taskmaster in every aspect. He hooked his women on drugs, beat them frequently into submission until their bodies and their wills were completely broken. On earth, he was complete in his brutality and greed, and was possessed with an insatiable lust. But here in his prison, he was forced to experience over and over again what he inflicted upon the women in his domain, only magnified to an unimaginable degree. He saw vividly the effect that his actions had on the souls of everyone he encountered during his lifetime, and this torture of regret ate at him continually. The most horrible-looking creatures mercilessly tore at his skin, continually mutilating him, ripping him apart from the crotch to the throat, and exposing him to unbelievable ridicule and humiliation. Over and over again, each torture exceeded the former in its barbarity. Screaming endlessly for help, he let out terrifying, ear-piercing screams, pleading with his torturers, which only intensified their hatred toward their trapped victim. At the end of each torture, his body was reduced to mere bits and pieces, then instantly he returned to normal, and his tortures began again.

"As we descended farther down toward the center of hell, the noise and total confusion continued in its escalation the deeper we went, and the tortures inflicted on the souls became more and more gruesome. I saw a man enclosed in one particular cell being tortured in the most atrocious way. He had lived in the early 1900's, was married and had four sons whom he repeatedly abused physically, sexually, and emotionally. This man was a violent alcoholic and very often drank away his wages without providing for his family. During his drunken rages, he spewed onto his wife and children horrific insults, cutting them down and destroying their spirit. He was sadistic beyond belief, and as a direct result, his youngest son committed suicide. His child having repented was safe in the arms of God, but this man was held responsible for the life cut short by his abuse. In this chamber, he was shackled in chains and was stretched upon a blackened stone table. He was being forced to drink a thick squalid liquid, which was poured into his mouth by a very large horrific-looking animal. He was forced to ingest huge amounts of it in recompense for his insatiable appetite for alcohol. His abdomen quickly distended, and you could see him being eaten by worms from the inside. Then he was beaten and smashed until he would vomit. The fluid expelled from him looked like molten lava, which burned and melted his flesh. He was mangled and crushed by the blows of these demons until he was reduced into to a slimy puddle of bones and liquefied flesh. Then immediately he was returned to normal, and his chains were released. He struggled to flee, and initially he thought he had escaped, but was captured again, toyed with and teased by his captors, and dragged back onto the table where it all began again. The fear expressed upon his face is something I will never forget. The insults hurled upon him were so foul and hateful, in a language that was so abhorrent, that I often have nightmares where I am forced to watch his tortures over and over. I had to turn away because it was awful to witness."

Alan paused and adjusted himself in the bed. "Every one of the souls I saw in hell understood exactly why they were there. You see, God doesn't put us into hell. We put ourselves there. Every soul at judgment sees with perfect clarity their life as God sees it. They then judge themselves in His light. There is no rebuttal when standing before God because their sinfulness before absolute purity cries out their judgment. Do you see? It is us, *our* actions, *our* words, *our* omissions, and ultimately, *our* total rejection of God's grace that decides our fate." Saying this, Alan tapped his finger to his breastbone over and over, as if he were accusing himself again. "Every soul, even up to the last moment of their life, is given the choice of accepting God or rejecting Him. The souls in hell are those that reject Him, His love, His grace, and most importantly, they reject His mercy, even after they have seen Him! Then they hurl themselves into this abyss because it is far worse for them to stand before God than to be in darkness!" Alan paused, shook his head, and looked up at me with such sadness in his eyes. "So many people believe that hell will be a big party, an orgy of sin. What they don't realize is that they will be completely and absolutely alone. The souls I saw imprisoned there were cognizant of no other person, only their demonic torturers. So besides pain and despair, they suffer an overwhelming and penetrating loneliness. This terrible loneliness is caused by their detachment from God, and it is so complete that the human tongue cannot express it in its fullness. It is, by far, the greatest of their tortures. This separation from God leaves an inner desolation that completely consumes them and is experienced immediately. Their judgment, their terrible judgment, is swift, and they flee from God and His justice and throw themselves headlong into hell. From that moment on, they are forever incapable of feeling or expressing love, only hatred. The regret that they do feel will never lead to repentance because their fate is sealed at their judgment and riveted in refusal, so their want of, or any desire for, forgiveness is impossible. Since their unrepentant offenses are to an infinite God, their sentence is therefore infinite. People don't get out of hell."

Tears welled up in Alan's eyes, and he reached up and wiped his tissue over them. With a short inhalation and an emotion-laden voice, he said, "It broke my heart to have seen so many souls there. Not only witnessing their pain, but remembering my own judgment as I stood before Jesus. You can't imagine how much sadness He feels, loving us so much as we turn our backs on Him. Can you imagine His sorrow as His children spit in His face and say, 'No, I don't want you? I would rather be in hell than to be anywhere near you?' Alan reached up, wiped his eyes again then paused and dropped his head to his chest as he sat deep in thought. "They call down upon themselves His justice and therefore His vengeance, and it is terrible." He reached over to his bedside table and took a drink. Placing it back on the table, he continued saying, "People should read Ezekiel 25:17, where it says, 'And I will execute great vengeance upon them, rebuking them in fury: and they shall know that I am the Lord, when I shall lay my vengeance upon them.'"

Alan paused for quite some time, then looked toward the end of his bed and began again. "Quickly we descended until we reached what appeared to be the bottom of a huge pit. In its center was an immense cell with doors as thick as they were tall. These doors opened at the command of St. Michael, and a sickening smoke spewed out, enveloping all that was around us. My angel raised his hand, and as we approached, it was instantly filled with a brilliant light. The walls were oozing and quivering with what appeared to be snakes and vermin of unearthly size that slithered and scurried away toward the darkness at the back of the cell. In the center was an immense throne that was made entirely of gold and silver coins, bouillon, and blocks and, although dull and tarnished, was heaped in piles, forming a basic throne shape, and it was huge. At its base were souls of humans, some with skin, some only bones, all in varying degrees of decay and covered with worms. When the bones were completely bare and all the flesh had decayed or had been eaten by the worms, they immediately became covered in skin, and it all started again, burning, rotting, digesting. These souls were completely immobile, and each moaned and quivered beneath the weight of this massive throne. From behind me, I felt a terrifying presence, a presence so completely evil and so full of hatred that I was frozen in place. I felt it approach me, its heat flowing over the back of my neck. So complete was its hatred of me that I felt this hatred cover me with an oppressive hopelessness. I instinctively knew who this was and knew that he was permanent in his state. Not only could he not alter his destiny, he would never desire it—ever. His damnation was cemented in complete and total opposition to God. He hated entirely all that God is, and therefore hated entirely all God had created." Alan paused for a time. "As I stood there, I felt him study me then slowly, he slithered around in front of me. I didn't want to look at him. His foul stench permeated my nostrils as I felt his gaze seeking out every part of my soul, searing it with his eyes, searching for every fault. He backed up, and my guardian angel told me to look. I lifted my head and in front of me was a creature so incredibly evil, so vile and full of hatred, that I cannot express it in its full enormity. He flopped himself down on the throne, causing moans from the corpses lying beneath it. He slammed his hoof-like foot swiftly into the mouth of the source of one of the complaints, twisting and crushing it deeper into the slimy ground. He was huge, as black as tar and glistened like glass. His slit fissured eyes were a tortured, deep reddish-black surrounded by an eerie glow that was penetrating and frightful. His huge horns were protruding from either side of his bulging forehead, curling back toward his shoulders and ending behind his back. His face was elongated at its base, serpentine and hideous in all of its features. Nothing can describe him because he resembles nothing of this earth. What I can't express enough is his hatred, and his hatred right then was focused at me. I could hear his filthy, debasing words enter my mind. I tried to reassure myself with what my angel had told me earlier, when another charge was hurled at me with increasing rapidity and force. Cunning and vulgar, his accusations filled me with uncertainty. This only escalated his assault, one after another, after another. All of it twisted, exaggerated, and after every word, I could hear him hiss, 'You belong to me! You will never belong to Him! You deserve to be here! You can never be forgiven for all of it! You are mine and have been mine all along!' Michael raised his hand, which stopped Satan's attack on me, and in a thunderous, majestic voice, Michael shouted, 'Enough!' A bright light emanated from my guides, growing brighter and brighter as I saw Satan cowering to get away from it. He started howling, hurling blasphemies at us with such a thunderous roar that the walls of this dungeon should have been shattered. Quickly and forcefully, we flew up and out of that pit. The gates slammed shut, and its huge bolts were rammed forcefully into their former position, enclosing its inhabitants forever. We flew upward, rocketing at an ever-increasing speed, and I could hear Satan's blasphemous screams slowly diminishing. Then instantly we were out of that horrible darkness and back into the light, far away from the heat and the stench of hell. I was so thankful to be out of that cesspool of filth that I wept. Clinging to my guardian angel, I thanked them both for taking me out of there. We came to a stop, and Michael turned to me and said, 'You have only seen a small glimpse of hell, do not forget it!' With that, my guides disappeared, and I was hurled again, this time on my own, through a very dark tunnel. When I opened my eyes, I was lying on my back with a tube in my mouth. My head spun, and my chest was in horrific pain as I attempted to breathe. I was confused and frightened and was unable to move my arms or legs. In this confusion, I thought maybe I had been shoved into that hole in the wall of hell. I became frantic and tried with all the strength I had to wiggle out of what was holding my arms and legs. Then I heard my doctor's voice explaining again to relax, that the surgery was over and that they were going to remove my breathing tube. I realized then that I was on earth and in the hospital, and I was so relieved to be there and not in hell." He sighed, reached over, and took another sip of water.

"Wow, Alan, what a story! So tell me, how has your life changed since that experience?"

"Well, nothing about my life is the same, and it changed the minute my breathing tube was out. I asked for a priest to come as soon as possible. I was frantic and told the nurses that they had to hurry up and get me a priest. None were available until the next day, and that night I didn't sleep at all. I hadn't been to confession since grade school and hadn't been to Mass since I was in high school. When the priest arrived the next day, I asked him to hear my confession. I fumbled with the words, not remembering how to begin, but he patiently talked me through it. It took three hours, but I confessed it all. When he gave me absolution, I couldn't stop crying, and I cried for an hour after he left. The following week I got out of the hospital, and after I recovered and got my strength back, I sat my wife down and I apologized to her for everything. Then I went to each one of my children, and I apologized to them because I had completely failed them. At first they refused, but eventually they did forgive me. We are very close now, and I've tried every day to show them how much I love them." He smiled. "It took Regina a long time because I was so rotten to her all of our married life. She wasn't convinced that I had really changed, but eventually she did forgive me, and we're together over fifty years now. Yes, she took this old sinner back, and may God be praised for that!" Alan looked down at his wedding band and twirled it around his finger with his right hand. After a short pause, he looked up from his hands and looked over at me. "I've spent every moment since then making it up to them and to Jesus. I pray all the time since that awful day, and I go every single day to Mass and Communion. Now we're dealing with this cancer. Regina's having a difficult time accepting the end so much more than I am. I know this disease has run its course, and I know I'm dying. I long for the day, but can't really share that with her, but I can't wait!"

He smiled over at me. "It's quite a story, isn't it? I can't tell you how many times I've told it, and every single time, I can't stop the tears because I almost didn't make it. I almost ended up permanently in that horrible place, and rightly so. But Jesus, in one act of unbelievable and undeserved mercy, changed it all, and I've spent every single day thanking Him for it. People need to realize that nothing is unforgivable because Jesus is bigger than any sin. But He can't forgive us if we are unwilling to ask for His forgiveness." Alan reached over and squeezed my hand. "All we have to do is love Him. How do you do that? You love the people you meet every day, whether it's your family or your co-workers, or in your case, your patients. Our command is to love everyone, especially the tyrant who hates us. Jesus didn't condemn the soldiers who put Him to death, did He? He was the prime example of how we are to treat everyone. It's so simple—difficult many times, yes, but simple. If I meet people who are only concerned about themselves, I am obligated before God to tell them the treacherous path they walk, so I tell them my story, the story of what will happen if they continue down the wrong road. Some accept it, some reject it, but the seed is still planted."

Alan proceeded to decline as the bleeding from his bladder continued. Not once, did any of us ever hear him complain. One evening, I arrived at work and immediately went in to check on him. He was drenched in sweat and was very pale, a sickly gray sort of pale. We wiped him down and changed his linens and his gown. When we were finished, he looked up at me and whispered, "It's almost over." I leaned over and hugged him, heartbroken that my friend was dying.

"God bless you, my dear friend," I whispered into his ear.

Alan smiled up at me and whispered, "I will pray for you when I am with my Jesus."

Alan soon became less responsive, so I phoned his wife and children to come in. They stood around his bed as he slipped into unconsciousness. His wife kept vigil near the head of his bed and never let go of his hand. She often kissed it, pressed his palm to her cheek just as she did the day we admitted him. His children, silent and calm in their grief, also stayed next to his bed. They were often heard softly singing or praying. Alan died peacefully at 3:00 AM.

Millie: An Invisible Companion

Millie arrived as a respite patient early one evening on a hot Monday in August. We went to meet her at the front door with a wheelchair. As she was being assisted out of her car, she looked over at us, flung her arms open wide, and yelled, "Are you girls ready for me?"

Millie was an eighty-six-year-old widow who was in hospice for end-stage cardiac disease. She had malfunctioning and diseased cardiac valves that were inoperable due to her other, very numerous comorbidities. Millie lived with her son, George, and his wife, in an in-law suite they added onto the main level of their home. George and his wife were heading off for vacation and felt it was unsafe for her to stay at home alone. A long-term diabetic, Millie's vision was poor, and with the fluid accumulation in her legs from her poorly functioning heart, it was nearly impossible for her to ambulate unassisted. She was a heavy set woman with short, cropped gray hair that was neatly set in a stiffly sprayed pile of curls on her head. She walked with the assistance of a walker but, for long distances, required a wheelchair. Dressed in a long purple-and-orange floral day dress, she hobbled from the car to the awaiting wheelchair. Once in the door, she opened her arms to all the awaiting staff and hugged every one of us. We settled Millie in to her room and sat her in a recliner, elevated her heavy fluid-filled legs, and set her bedside table next to her. After arranging her things to her specifications, I went to fetch a cup of iced water as she requested. When I returned to her room to deliver the cup, I found her talking with someone invisible to me. When I entered the room and set her cup next to her, she looked up and smiled at me and said, "I guess you caught me, didn't you?"

"Just because I can't see who you're talking to, doesn't mean they aren't there," I answered, smiling down at her and patting her shoulder.

"Well, there is only one, and his name is Gabe, and he's been with me for the past six months or so. He doesn't frighten me like the first time I saw him." She chuckled softly.

"Would you mind telling me about that?" I asked as I pulled up a chair to sit next to her.

"Well, sure if you want to listen. I am not sure if you knew, but my husband died about a year ago, and I was going through a terrible time dealing with the loss. After fifty-eight years of marriage, I lost the true love of my life. You have no idea how that devastated me. Never before had I gone through something so difficult, and it was nearly impossible for me to go on. One night I was lying in bed, and I was on the point of ending it all. I was exhausted carrying such a deep sadness within me that I had actually decided to do it the next day—you know, kill myself. I went to bed that night and reached over and turned off my bedroom light, and when I looked at the foot of my bed to pull my covers up over myself, there was this figure standing at the foot of my bed. He was wearing a pale gray outfit and was holding a book in one hand and a long pen with a golden nib in the other. Scared the hell out of me! I sat up in the bed and asked him who he was and what he wanted. He looked at me with deep, sad eyes and shook his head. I knew what he meant by that, so I told him that I wouldn't do it, I wouldn't kill myself. He wrote something down in his book and closed it, crossed both arms in front of him, and bowed his head. Then poof! He disappeared. I've been seeing him on and off since then. My daughter-in-law thinks I'm a loon, but he's as real and as solid to look at as you are sitting right here." She reached over and placed her hand on my forearm.

"Does he ever speak to you, Millie?" I asked.

"No, but I feel great comfort when he is here. He's like my guardian angel. When my world gets disrupted and is up in a whirl, he shows up, and his presence calms me down. I didn't really want to come here because . . . well, it's just not home. No offense to you, you understand, but I think everyone really would rather stay at home, don't you think?" Millie sighed.

"Yes, I do, but we'll take good care of you, and we're very happy to have you with us."

"Well, I'm glad to hear that, but that's who I was talking to when you caught me. It's okay if you think I'm crazy, it doesn't bother me. I know what I see and what I feel when he's here. I've nicknamed him Gabe—you know, like the angel Gabriel?" She beamed a grin, revealing her toothless gums.

"Gabriel's a very good name. We're happy to have both of you with us." I smiled back at her. "Is there anything else I can get for you?"

"No, you've been very kind." After making sure her call bell was within reach, I left to check on my other patients.

Millie stayed with us the whole five days and was a gem of a lady, congenial, patient, and a joy to care for. The morning of her discharge, I went into her room to say good-bye, as I was leaving for the day.

"Millie, I do hope you will come stay with us again. It was an absolute pleasure to take care of you." Millie reached up from her chair, opening her arms to welcome a hug. I leaned over and hugged her. "God bless you, sweet lady," I whispered in her ear.

"God bless you too, my dear. We will never forget you." Beaming her toothless grin, her eyes twinkled beneath a halo of wrinkles. "Will we, Gabe? I hope you wrote her name down too," she said, looking over her left shoulder at her "friend." "Gabe keeps a list of people I remember in my prayers. Keeps me from having to remember so many names. This old head of mine! Peoples' names go in and fall right through the holes in my noggin!" She laughed, throwing her head back, revealing her upper gums as well.

"Do come back and stay with us, we really enjoyed having you," I said as I took her hands in mine and squeezed them gently.

"Oh, honey, that isn't in the cards I'm afraid. My time here is coming to an end. But I will never forget any of you, and please, thank everyone who helped me will you?" she said as she patted my hand in hers.

"I absolutely will."

Two months after her stay with us, we read her obituary in the newspaper. Her son stopped by and delivered a beautiful bouquet of flowers and told us that she had passed peacefully in her sleep.

Jonathan: Permission to Leave

Jonathan came into our unit from the nearby hospital with end-stage lung disease. Jonathan was only fifty-eight years old, and had been married to his wife, Pat, for thirty-eight years. Jonathan was a long-time smoker who had developed pneumonia requiring hospitalization. The pneumonia had overtaken his lungs and responded poorly to all antibiotics. He had developed an abscess in his lower right lung, which had grown so rapidly that he ended up intubated and on a ventilator for a time. After several procedures to drain the pus, his lungs became so compromised and fibrotic that his prognosis was very poor. A final cat scan revealed that the disease had progressed so virulently that he was given a very short time to live. After a hospice consult was obtained, Jonathan was transferred to our hospice for end-of-life care. The ambulance stretcher rolled through the doors, and Jonathan was sitting upright and in obvious respiratory distress. After quickly settling him in the bed, we started SQ lines to quickly give him some medication to ease his air hunger. Jonathan's wife, obviously distraught with worry and grief, accompanied him. Jonathan's son, Jason, and daughter, Kay, also arrived and appeared disheveled and exhausted. Kay took me aside and said, "I am a nurse, and I saw those cat scans. It's very bad, and I can't believe he has hung on as long as he has. Mom is a mess and is in complete denial . . . just wanted to let you know."

Pat was very doting and stayed close to Jonathan and asked many questions regarding medications and his plan of care. Jonathan settled down a bit after the first dose of medication, but could not tolerate having his head lowered for any time at all. I added medications to help with his congestion, but informed Pat and Kay that sometimes the medications aren't as effective when the congestion is caused by pus or large amounts of fluid in the lung. I added nebulizers to help ease some of the wheezing he exhibited. Despite all efforts, Jonathan declined quickly. He required medication adjustments, and it was difficult to watch how he struggled despite all interventions.

"Don't leave me, Jonnie, I'm not ready. Please, please hang on," Pat was often heard telling Jonathan. Hour after hour, Jonathan struggled as we did our best to ease his suffering. I signaled to Pat and Kay to meet me outside Jonathan's room. I didn't want to talk over him, but felt the need to speak with them alone regarding Jonathan's steady decline.

"Pat, I can't imagine how much pain this is causing you, but you can see that nothing we are doing is helping Jon, and he's declining quickly," I said as consolingly as I could.

"I know, I know there isn't anything else that can be done for him, but I can't face losing him," she whispered as tears streamed down her face.

"His anxiety and his struggling with every breath will soon become more than he can bear, and he will tire out, and I think we're at that turning point. He is getting tired now, and I fear he won't be here much longer," I said softly as I touched her hand.

"I see that, but is there anything else you can give him to help him keep fighting?" She glanced up at me with a quiet desperation spreading over her face.

"No, Pat, I'm sorry there is nothing else we can do. He may need your permission though," I said meeting her eyes with mine.

"What do you mean?"

"Well, I've heard you telling him not to leave, to hang on because you're not ready."

"Yes, that's true, I'm not ready, but I can't stand to see him struggling either," she said softly, as she wiped her tear-soaked eyes.

"No good husband wants to leave his wife if he knows she won't be okay. You may need to tell him that it's okay, reassure him that you will be strong. Tell him that you know he's tired and that you don't want him to suffer any longer. He may be waiting to hear those words before he can leave. I know this is very, very difficult to do."

"Oh no . . . do you think I made it worse?" she asked as she inhaled abruptly, stifling a sob.

"Oh, no, dear, I don't think you made it worse, but it is very obvious that you love him very much. But a gentleman won't leave without permission."

Pat broke down and sobbed. "I don't know if I can do this. I don't want him suffering anymore . . . but I don't want him to leave me." Wiping her tears, she looked up and smiled at me. "You know, as soon as that came out of my mouth, I see how ridiculous I sound." She wadded the tissue in half and wiped her eyes again.

"No, not ridiculous, not at all . . . just a grieving wife," I reassured her.

"I understand, I'll give him permission." Pat reached over and grabbed Kay's hand, then with the other hand, reached over and grabbed mine. "Will you come with me?"

"Absolutely!" we both chimed in unison.

We turned and walked back toward Jonathan's room. Melody, the nursing assistant also standing nearby, nodded in agreement. We approached Jonathan's bed, and his eyes were half-opened as he struggled with each inhalation. Kay and Pat approached the bed, and Jonathan's son, Jason, stood near them. I lowered the side rails to let Pat get nearer to her husband. Pat reached over toward Jonathan as he turned his head toward her. She placed both hands on his cheeks and looked deeply into his eyes. Leaning over, she gently kissed his forehead, both cheeks, and his mouth, and with eyes full of tears she said, "Jonnie, it's okay, it's okay to go. I love you, and I'll be okay. Jason and Kay will help me."

"Yes, Dad, we will," Jason said as he and Kay approached the other side of the bed to get closer to their father.

"I love you, Jonnie, I love you," Pat whispered as she covered him in kisses. Almost immediately, Jonathan relaxed and his color immediately grew pale. Tears welled up in my eyes, and Melody leaned near me, also full of emotion and whispered, "Oh my, look at that!" as she squeezed my elbow. Jonathan kept his eyes fixed on Pat, and their eyes embraced each other with such a look of love that it was difficult not to cry, witnessing this beautiful and tender good-bye. Jonathan's shoulders stopped heaving, and his furrowed brow relaxed.

Kay came around the other side of the bed and whispered into Jonathan's ear, "I love you, Daddy! I love you!"

Jason approached behind Kay as she ducked out of the way, and Jason tearfully whispered into Jonathan's ear, "I love you, Dad. Don't worry, I'll look out for Mom. You know I will. You were a great dad, I love you."

Pat kept her hands on either side of Jonathan's face, caressing his cheeks and his temples. Large tears flowed down her face as she attempted a smile. Two small tears seeped out of Jonathan's eyes as his breathing slowed. His eyes quickly grew dull, and his breathing became shallow and agonal in nature, and slowed significantly. Thirty seconds passed and another agonal breath. Jonathan inhaled and let out a long congested sigh and stopped breathing; his chest became silent and still. Pat kissed his eyes shut and placed her face next to his and began to sob. Kay stepped aside as I approached the bed. I placed my stethoscope on Jonathan's chest and listened to the silence.

"I'm very sorry," I whispered as I pulled away from the bedside to allow his family to say their final good-byes. Kay leaned in and sobbed, kissing her father's face, tears streaming from her eyes and dropping to his forehead. Then she retreated from the bed and walked over and stood next to us.

"What now?" she asked as she wiped her face with a tissue.

"I'll give you time alone with your father. When you're ready, I can call the funeral home for you." I reached over and touched her shoulder as she leaned her head onto me, and I hugged her gently.

"I'm so sorry, Kay. Take all the time you need. Just let me know when you're ready."

"Okay, thank you." She sniffed into her tissue.

After some time, Pat, Jason, and Kay approached the desk. Pat looked over at me and smiled and quietly said, "We're ready." She sighed. "We don't want to be here when they take him, so we're going to go ahead and leave now."

I came around the desk and hugged her, again expressing my sympathy. Pat whispered, "I know he's in a better place, and I'm happy to see that he's at peace."

She wiped her eyes and smiled. "We had a good life together, and I'll miss him terribly, but I'm relieved that he's done with the struggle."

George: Afraid to Die

At sixty-eight years old, a diagnosis of stage IV prostate cancer hit George hard. After every conceivable treatment and experimental therapies, the metastatic sites showed no improvement. A large tumor invaded his bladder, and he was unable to void due to the encroachment of the cancer near the base of his bladder, blocking the urethra. A supra-pubic catheter (above the pubic bone) was placed while he was in the hospital to relieve the urinary retention he was having. George was discharged from the hospital and sent home with home hospice. Having significant bone pain that was unrelieved by oral morphine, George arrived requiring a PCA pump to be started to control his pain. His wife arrived with him, and as soon as we got him settled, she went home for the night. She was weary, disheveled, and appeared completely exhausted.

George was a retired plumber and had a wife and two grown sons. George was a tall man, six feet four inches, and was solid in build. He had thin gray hair and deep-set hazel eyes. He had a beautiful smile and perfect teeth for a man his age. Once I assessed George, I hooked his PCA pump up to his port and gave him an initial bolus. Several dosage adjustments were required before his pain began to diminish.

"Am I going to die here?" he asked with anxiety in his voice.

"Not necessarily, George. We send plenty of people back home. You're here just to get your pain under control, and once that's accomplished and we have you on the right recipe so to speak, then we can send you home with this pump." I smiled over at George, but he was obviously anxious. "What's the matter George?" I asked, but he only shook his head. "Do you want to talk about anything?" I asked as I placed the pain pump back into its zippered case.

"I don't want to die, I'm not ready for it. I've got a lot to live for, and I can't believe this cancer hasn't budged. I've done everything the doctors told me to, and it pisses me off that nothing has touched it." He turned his head away and ran his fingers through his hair, folded his hands together and rested them on his lap.

"Are you scared?" I asked when George's chin began to quiver. He reached over and took a sip of water from his over-bed table.

"No, I'm not scared . . . I'm terrified," he whispered. "I never thought I would be, but when you're facing it head-on, it's terrible. I've got so much that I need to finish and things I haven't done . . . and there's so much that I should have done," he sighed.

"Do you want to talk about that?" I asked consolingly.

"You don't have time to sit here and listen to me," he grumbled.

"Actually, George, I do have time. It helps when you have someone to talk to, and I love to listen." I reached over and slid a chair close to his bed and sat down.

"I don't know. I go back and forth so much, and you can't tell me what to expect because I doubt you've ever died," he said, running his hands through his hair again.

"No, that's true, but I've taken care of plenty of people who have died that came back and told me about it. What scares you the most?" I asked, and leaned in to give him my full attention.

"I don't know. When I look back on my life, I should have spent more time with my family. I've worked like a dog my whole life, and there were so many times I chose my job over them. If I could take it all back, I would have savored that time with my wife and kids, and let the job wait. I mean who needs to work seven days a week, every holiday, including Christmas? Ridiculous." He sighed and fiddled with the bedrail to lower his head. He appeared very uncomfortable, and as it was time for an increase, I picked up his pump and adjusted his dosage up another few milligrams. I offered George medication for anxiety, but he refused. He was up and down during the night because of restlessness and feeling "like I've had too much coffee." He finally relented, and I gave him some Ativan, which helped tremendously. After that, he would ask for it now and again because it worked so well for him.

After a few days, I came back in to work and went in to see George. The chaplain had been in every day to speak with him regarding his anxiety about death, which really helped but did not take it away completely. The medication adjustments and intermittent Ativan had significantly diminished his symptoms, and he was scheduled to go home the following morning. As time allowed during my shift, I often checked on George, and if he was awake and wanted to talk, I would sit by his bed and we would talk about everything from his family, to his faith, and even his fears. When asked directly about his fears, he was much more open to discussing the details of them.

"I guess it's natural to have a certain amount of fear about death. The chaplain explained that everyone has a fear of it to a certain degree. I really think mine is worse than most people. What if I'm not good enough? What if I didn't make the cut?" George openly vented about his desire to have more time and his many regrets verbalized in the I-wish-I-would-haves and if-I-had-only statements that seemed to reoccur throughout our conversations. I did my best to listen and reassure. We spoke of God's mercy and how there is no limit to it when we ask.

"George, you have children, right? If either of your boys had done something wrong, but then came to you full of regret and asked you to forgive them, would you say, 'Get away from me, you don't deserve my forgiveness'?"

"Heavens no! I would forgive them immediately."

"Why would God, who loves us more than we could ever comprehend, who is love and mercy in its most perfect sense, deny His children forgiveness if they asked?" George looked over at me and smiled. "He is the perfect Father after all, isn't He?" I added as I smiled at him.

Just then, Julie came rushing into the room, saying, "You need to come quickly." I left immediately and tended to the other patient as requested. By the time I finished, when I checked on George, he had turned himself on his side and had gone to sleep. He was discharged the following morning, and I thought I wouldn't see him again.

Three weeks later, at around 10:00 PM, I received a call from the field nurse requesting a bed for a patient in terrible terminal agitation. When I heard that it was George, I quickly readied a bed for him, and within the hour, he was transferred in. When the ambulance stretcher rounded the corner, George was sitting up in bed, pale and diaphoretic. After getting him into the bed, I began my assessment, when George grabbed my arm and whispered with terrible anxiety in his voice, "Help me, please help me." I checked his PCA pump and adjusted his medication, then quickly inserted a SQ line and gave him an initial dose of Ativan. George was quivering, in pain, and terribly anxious. Once the necessary adjustments were made, and after several more medications, it finally caught up with him, and he began to settle down. His breathing relaxed and his quivering eased. Several times during the night he would rebound and become agitated but responded beautifully to the medications provided.

At around 3:00 AM, the nursing assistant and I were making rounds and found George scooting toward the end of the bed. "Where are you going, George?" I asked as we carefully lifted his legs back into the bed. We scooted him up, but he didn't answer. I stayed with him to make sure he was safe, when he sat up in bed and looked at the wall toward the foot of his bed. His eyes opened wide, and his jaw dropped. He stared, transfixed on that particular area of the wall for probably two full minutes. He smiled slowly, and I asked him, "George, what do you see?"

After a moment, his eyes met mine and he said, "Tell them all, Kelley, tell all of your patients that there's nothing to be afraid of. Tell them that it's beautiful over there." George reached both his hands up and took me by the upper arms. "Tell them that there's nothing to be afraid of, that God . . ." George's voice broke with emotion and tears welled up in his eyes, then he said, "Tell them that God loves them and is waiting for them, and He loves us so much." George's eyes moved past me and looked again at the wall. "Tell them that it's so beautiful, so beautiful . . ." George relaxed back, and we pulled him up higher in the bed. He stared at the wall for quite some time and then drifted off to sleep.

George never required another dose of Ativan for anxiety, and his pain pump remained at the same dose for the next twenty-four hours. George was then transferred back home, as his wish was to die at home with his family. Three days later, we received a call from his wife saying that George died peacefully, surrounded by his family.

Douglas: A Demon Within

Douglas was admitted into the hospital early Friday morning in a pain crisis related to metastatic cancer. Although the report from the hospital documented it as gastric and esophageal cancer, in speaking with his oncologist, he stated that he believed that its origin was pancreatic.

"The way this has exploded, it is acting very much like a virulent pancreatic cancer. Since he won't let us biopsy him, we did scans which lit up like the Fourth of July. We placed him on a pain pump, but his prognosis is very poor—he has very little time."

Douglas arrived Saturday afternoon to our hospice awake and alert, and according to the day-shift nurse reporting to me, was "a nasty cuss." Having to incrementally increase his pain pump upon arrival, she had finally gotten his pain pretty much under control. When I started my rounds, my first stop was his room. Lying in the bed was an infirm, emaciated man who looked years beyond his documented age of fifty-one. Had I not looked at his chart, I would have guessed he was in his mid-seventies. Douglas was skin-and-bones, and had a deep yellow-green tinged jaundice so indicative of end-stage disease. His hollow and sunken eyes were weary-looking from a distance. As I approached his bed, Douglas looked up at me and snapped, "What the f—— do you want? Why can't you sons-o'-bitches leave me alone?" He glared at me.

"I'm just coming on duty, and I have to check you over. When I'm finished, I'll leave you alone if that is what you want, but I have to at least assess you." I placed my hands on his side rail.

"Hurry the hell up," he snarled.

Douglas was incredibly thin and had significant muscle wasting. Each rib was clearly defined, and it was easy to see his heart pounding through his chest wall. His carotid arteries on either side of his neck were pulsating visibly. His abdomen was distended, firm, and no bowel sounds were appreciated. His skin was taut and shiny over his abdomen, while the skin on his thighs and arms was loose and sagging. His ankles were edematous, and his feet and knees were mottled. (Mottling is a purplish blotchy pattern seen on the skin as death approaches. It usually begins in the feet and works its way up the body.) The nail beds on his fingers were a dusky pale blue.

"Douglas, how is your breathing? You look a little short of breath," I said as calmly as I could.

"I don't give a damn about my breathing, and neither should you. If you're done, get the f—— out of my room, and leave me alone."

"Are you in pain?" I asked as I checked through the pain pump to see how many times he pushed the button for additional pain meds.

"I'm always in pain," he growled.

Seeing that he had pushed it quite frequently, I looked at him and said, "I'm going to increase your dosage, and we'll see if that helps."

"'We'll see if that helps,'" he mimicked in a whiny, taunting tone.

"Here's your call bell, let me know if that adjustment doesn't work. We can always go up."

"Fine, now leave!" he squealed as he yanked the call bell from my hand.

I left the room and thought that there had to be something I'd missed. An hour later, when I finished my rounds, I checked on

Douglas and adjusted his pain medicine again as he was still in obvious discomfort. I went back to the desk and grabbed his chart and began to read his history. Abandoned as a child, in and out of foster homes, bouts with the law as a teenager, jail, and substance abuse. I dropped my chart when I heard the most terrifying howl. I bolted up and ran down the hall toward his room and found him lying in bed, his arms down at his side, and he was screaming and howling like an animal.

"Douglas!" I called out to him as I reached over and put my hands on his chest. "What's the matter?" I shook him gently.

With a deep growl and spit flying from his mouth, he jerked his head toward me and said slowly and forcefully in a voice completely otherworldly, "Get away from me, you filthy bitch!"

His tone was gruesome in its hatred, and the hair stood up on my neck. My arms immediately erupted in goose bumps, and my knees began to shake, as I had never heard anything so terrifying in all my life. Douglas lifted his head and started banging it repeatedly onto his pillow, eyes rolled up to the ceiling.

"Are you in pain, Douglas?" I asked, thinking, was this his reaction to pain? Who knows? I was dumbfounded by his hatred of me, of the nursing assistants, of everyone who had any contact with him.

Laughing a terrible, deep belly cackle, he looked my direction and smiled a wide, clenched smile. Keeping his eyes on mine, his head rolled in a circle. In a sinister voice, he said, "Iiiitttt . . . nnnne-verrrr . . . sssstopsssss!"

Since it had been an hour since the last increase, I removed the pump from the zippered case and began increasing his dose, when *click!* The lights went out. The only thing illuminating the room was the glow from the screen of the pump I held in my hands. I quickly titrated his dose up and could feel the adrenalin hit my veins as my fingers had begun to tingle. I quickly zippered the pump into its case and turned to leave the room. As I approached the door, the lights clicked back on, and I turned around and looked at Douglas. He was still lying flat in the bed, but his head was upright with his chin pressing into his chest, and he was smiling, a sickening grin exposing his decaying teeth.

"Still scared of the dark, I see?" he whispered, and began to cackle with ever-increasing volume. Slowly he tilted his head to the side, his ear down where his chin would normally sit, as the bones in his neck crunched. My knees buckled as another wave of adrenalin hit, and I quickly left the room and closed the door. Anyone who is close to me knows that I am afraid of the dark. I have been since childhood, and it's something I've never been able to overcome. I don't readily admit it to strangers, and nobody in the hospice knew this. When I left the room, I hastily walked down the hall. I was visibly shaking as the nursing assistant Janice came around the corner from another patient's room. She walked over to me and grabbed my arm.

"Are you okay? You're as white as a sheet! What happened, are you sick?" I proceeded to tell her about what happened, how his voice changed, the weird cackling he was doing, and how he was rolling and twisting his head. I explained how the lights went off by themselves, what he said, and how he was completely accurate.

"There's something evil in that room, Janice, and I don't want to go in there alone anymore. You shouldn't go in alone either. I increased his pain pump, and hopefully that will last him awhile. I need to sit down." I went around the desk and sat at the computer. My heart was pounding, and sweat was dripping down my back. After taking a few moments to collect myself, Janice and I repositioned the other two patients in the unit. Although both were unresponsive, I was thankful that no family members were in the unit tonight. An hour later, I checked in on Douglas because it had been almost an hour and I had to make sure his pain was decreasing. When I peeked in his room, he was lying in bed, eyes closed and facing the window. He didn't stir when I opened the door, and since he was peaceful and breathing easily, I shut the door. I continued to check on him throughout the night, but since he could reposition himself, we only checked his breathing and to see if he was soiled or in pain. At five in the morning, Janice and I went in to check on him, and the odor in the room indicated that he was incontinent of stool. We prepared our things and rolled him toward me so Janice could begin to clean him up. He looked up at me, scowling at the Miraculous Medal that was dangling from my neck.

"What are you trying to prove with that fancy little talisman?" he mocked as he reached up and flicked it with his fingernail.

"I wear it for me, and not for you, so I'd appreciate it please if you kept your hands to yourself." I tucked my necklace into my scrub top. He rolled his eyes and snickered, then let loose a deep drawn-out belch. I diverted my eyes, rarely making eye contact with him. We rolled him on the other side, and I finished cleaning the black foul-smelling stool from his skin. I pulled the dirty sheets through, wadded them up, and laid them in the bag on the chair. I pulled his clean sheets and pads through and tucked them in.

"How's your pain, Douglas?" I asked as we finished up.

"As I said, I'm always in pain," he said sarcastically.

"I'm going to adjust your pump up again, okay?"

"Do whatever the f—— you want to, you filthy c——, makes no difference to me."

As I adjusted his pain pump, Janice looked over at him and said, "You watch your mouth, young man. No need to be calling us filthy names when we just cleaned stool off your bum." She shoved the dirty linens into a large plastic bag. Douglas erupted once more into a brief fit of condescending laughter.

"And who are you?" he chided.

"My name is Janice, the one who just wiped your bum. Now be nice," she said in a rather reprimanding tone.

"Ah, Janissssssss!" Then he whispered, "I know exactly who you are! That was a little girl by the way . . . remember? Oh, don't recall? August 17, 1981, in that filthy hole on Barton Street?" I could see Janice stiffen up and glare at him. He stared up at her with a filthy grin on his face. Then in a sing-song taunting tease, he said, "Itty-bitty chopped up girl, arms and legs sucked up in a whirl." He made slurping, sucking sounds and stuck his tongue out at her, flicking it like a snake. Janice grabbed the linen bag and stormed out of the room. "Run away, Janissssss! Ha-ha-ha!" he howled, as if in delighted triumph. I left the room and found Janice sitting on a chair in the med room, visibly upset.

"Janice, don't listen to that crazy fool."

"No, no, he knows exactly what he's talking about!" As tears welled up in her eyes, she looked up at me with her lips pursed together.

"What is it, Janice? What?" I asked as I squatted down in front of her, grabbing her hand reassuringly.

"I got pregnant at seventeen and had an abortion," she blurted out, and in the same breath, she added, "Oh my god, nobody knows that!" She stood up and leaned on the countertop. "How could he know such a thing? And he knew the date, the address, and the year, for god's sake!" Tears rolled down her face as she clenched her fists together. "I tell you, he's got the devil in him, there's simply no other explanation!"

"Maybe so, Janice." I stood up and leaned next to her on the counter.

"How'd he know you were afraid of the dark, huh? I never knew that about you, but he did! I'm not going in there anymore, I tell you." Then pounding her hand on the cupboard, she said, "They can fire me!"

"Janice, he creeps me out too, but we can't *not* go in there. We only have a little over an hour left. We'll go in together, always together, okay?"

"I'm not going in there again. If he needs something, he can jolly well wait until security gets here. I tell you, I'm not going in there until security is here."

At six thirty in the morning, we checked on him again. His head was facing the door, and his piercing eyes were staring at us. I went in to check on him and found him incontinent of stool again. Janice phoned security, and they arrived very quickly because only then would she enter the room. As we hurried to finish the job, he continued taunting us, telling us things about ourselves that nobody knew: sins committed during our lives that were dead-on, even moments of impatience, anger, pride, impure thoughts with specifics. He continued on and on, spewing back at us our sins over a lifetime, many we had forgotten. As he spoke, his eyes remained fixed on us, but his head rolled around and around. He belched and growled in between questions directed at us. Janice attempted to answer, and I looked at her and quickly shook my head, telling her not to engage him. When we finished and were leaving the room, we could hear him cackle. We both looked in his direction, and he stuck out his long black-tinged tongue, flicking it in and out. His facial expression sent shivers through both of us. Janice grabbed my elbow and hurried me out the door, pulling it shut behind us.

Never in my life have I been so frightened, and never have I been confronted head-on with something so incredibly evil and hateful. When we reported off to the oncoming shift, we told them what had happened, but I left out the details, not wanting to divulge Janice's secret. I figured if she wanted to reveal it, it was her secret to reveal. Janice instead blurted out the whole story, breaking down as tears flowed from her eyes. She told them everything, and their response was typical of hospice personnel—they all hugged and consoled her.

I found myself praying for him on the drive home that morning. I remember telling God that I didn't know what his issue was, whether it was spiritual or psychological or both, but I begged God to have mercy on him nonetheless. Attempting sleep that morning was difficult as I could still hear him hissing Janice's name and could see his bulging eyes glaring at me while his head rolled around. I woke up several times that day with bad dreams. When I went back to work that night, I was surprised that he had died that morning. The day-shift nurse reported that his death was quite a struggle. He reportedly started to vomit, and it was dark-black, probably old blood, from the tumor in his gut. He reportedly hissed, "The appetizer before the meal." She reported that he howled and screamed like an animal at a slaughterhouse.

"In the thirty years I've been doing this, I've never seen a more awful death," the day-shift nursing assistant piped in.

Janice had called out of work saying she 'couldn't come in due to lack of sleep,' so I texted her telling her that he had died that morning. She came in at eleven o'clock and pulled me into a hug when we saw each other.

"If he was still here, I was planning on calling out every night until he was gone." She whispered to me, "I just couldn't bring myself to take care of him again." She let go and looked at me, her eyes glistening with tears.

I'm not here to judge him, but I hope and pray that he found peace in the end. Hopefully, he turned to God even if it was at the last second of his life. I believe wholeheartedly that God's mercy is offered to all of us, even up until the last second, the last heartbeat, the last breath.

About the Author

Kelley Jankowski has been a registered nurse for over 30 years. She started her career in critical care and then entered the field of hospice nursing. "I cared for a little lady who asked me if she could do anything for me. I thought this a sweet request given that she was bed-bound and unable to care for herself. I asked her that when she got to the other side and met God face to face, to please pray for me. My brother Patrick asked if that was a common request I made of my patients, and it is. He commented that if all of my patients over the years remembered that request, then surely I have an army in Heaven praying for me." Kelley, married and the mother of six children, resides with her husband, Ronald in Maryland.

CPSIA information can be obtained
at www.ICGtesting.com
Printed in the USA
LVOW07s1930090118
562393LV00003B/489/P